Finding Memories, Tracing Routes

Chinese Canadian Family Stories

**Chinese Canadian Historical Society
of British Columbia**

加華歷史協會

Chinese Canadian Historical Society of British Columbia
Vancouver, British Columbia, Canada
http://www.cchsbc.ca

Editing and book design by Brandy Liên Worrall.
Main contents set in Cochin.

Photograph credits for front cover images, from top to bottom: Gail
Yip, Dan Seto, Candace Yip, Belinda Hung, Shirley Chan, Hayne Wai,
Roy Mah (Kathy Arnsdorf), Ken Yip.

All images and photographs herein used with permission by
respective authors.   .

ISBN 978-1-84728-184-5

TABLE OF CONTENTS

"Writing multicultural histories that include everyone requires ordinary families and individuals to write their own stories as essential components. This volume gives us an excellent start on the journey to recover Chinese Canadian history in British Columbia. It also provides a superb model of the use of writing workshops to develop personal history-writing skills."

~DR. EDGAR WICKBERG

Founding President
Chinese Canadian Historical
Society of British Columbia

This volume is dedicated to Edgar Wickberg, whose vision and leadership created the Chinese Canadian Historical Society of British Columbia, and who has tirelessly devoted much of his long and distinguished career to the study of Chinese Canadian history.

We cannot decide from whom we want to descend. Our parents and grandparents have made that decision for us. We are who we are because of our families. Most of us know quite a lot about our parents, less about our grandparents, and almost nothing at all about the generations that came before them. Yet it is their genes that form us and their experiences that make it possible for us to be here today. Our families are the basis of who we are, and it is by learning about our inheritance that we come to know ourselves.

Two of the best ways to trace our roots are through memories and images. A handful of us will have ancestors in the history books as they are usually written, and a few others turn up in newspapers, but most of our families enter the written record only as snapshots in time—a marriage, a death, a census enumeration. It is the memories we have kept alive and the photographs safely tucked away that give the entryway to our inheritance. These are the two fundamental building blocks taking us back in time.

Sometimes we need a little push to take up the challenge. The inaugural Family History Writing Workshop sponsored by the Chinese Canadian Historical Society of British Columbia in the spring of 2006 gave eight men and women the opportunity to explore the potential in memories and images for finding out about ourselves and, most importantly, the rewards that come from doing so.

The eight stories that grew out of the workshop belie the easy excuse that the passage of time makes it too late for us to trace our roots. It's never too late, but then again it's never too early. Rather than lamenting what has been lost, we want to begin, as the eight writers do, with our own memories and with surviving photographs. It is from such beginnings that we can track down any newspaper accounts and documents traditionally seen as more factual and trustworthy. What the writers discovered was, of course, that memories and images often belie the supposed truth to be found in written records, for the most part created by the dominant society to maintain itself.

The writers have each crafted something far more valuable than the usual family tree. By telling a story that combines aspects of their family's history with their own search for understanding, starting with their own memories of parents and grandparents, the writers empower readers to begin a similar journey toward understanding.

The importance of the eight stories goes beyond the families themselves. We need to be particularly grateful to the writers for their willingness to share slices of lives that have up to now been hidden away in the shadows of Canadian history. Each of the stories contributes immeasurably to our understanding of the Chinese presence in Canada, and especially in British Columbia. The Chinese were among the first newcomers to British Columbia, yet we know very little about their everyday lives. It is indicative of the lingering conceit in the dominant society that we have paid more attention to attitudes toward the Chinese than about the ways in which individuals and families have survived and thrived through time—that is, until now.

Arrivals from China, both directly and via California, were among the earliest and most intrepid participants in the gold rush beginning in British Columbia in 1858 and then in the construction of the transcontinental rail line across Canada completed in the mid-1880s. The eight stories give us glimpses into both these events. Shirley Chan's great-grandfather came to mine gold in 1879 and, not striking it rich, worked on the railway. Ken Yip's grandfather, Yip Chung Ben, was just sixteen when in 1882 he and his partner Dennis Quong began placer mining at Wild Horse Creek in the East Kootenays.

Rail line complete, the racism of the dominant society in Canada came to the fore with a vengeance. At the time British Columbia entered the Canadian Confederation in 1871, between one in five and one in six of its non-Aboriginal population had been Chinese. Three years later the new provincial government took away their right to vote, which meant they could not enter the professions of law, pharmacy, or accountancy, work for the government, or pre-empt land. Even though almost all of the Chinese in Canada continued to live in British Columbia, away from the centre of power, on the franchise being centralized in 1885 the Dominion government followed suit. The same year, it introduced a head tax of $50 on new arrivals from China, raised to $100 in 1900 and to $500 three years later. No other immigrant group was similarly targeted.

Despite the restrictions, Chinese continued to arrive until being prohibited from doing so altogether in 1923. The reasons 81,000 men, women, and children paid the head tax in order to come to Canada were often traumatic: Candace Yip, for instance, characterizes her grandfather as a political refugee, having been from a very young age on the wrong side after a military rebellion.

The easing of the immigration ban from 1948 initiated another round of immigration that continues into the present day. Hayne Wai's and Roy Mah's families were among those arriving in the 1950s. Hayne Wai's family joined grandparents already in British Columbia; for Roy Mah's parents it meant leaving behind in China everything they had spent a lifetime working for and beginning anew. From a low of 24,000 in 1951, the number of Canadians born in China grew to 635,000 by 2001. The total of Chinese descent went from 32,500 to over a million. Whereas two-thirds of Canadians of Chinese descent lived in British Columbia up to the time of the Second World War, just a third did so in 2001.

The eight stories point to how essential the Chinese have been to the Canadian economy, particularly to the resource and service sectors to which they were long restricted. Joe Hop Lee worked as a houseboy, chopped wood, and sold produce from his orchard and garden. Yip Chung Ben did so well in gold mining that he opened a general store in the East Kootenays boomtown of Cranbrook. On arriving in the 1890s, Gail Yip's great-grandparents established a labour contracting business in New Westminster's Chinatown, as the areas in which many of the Chinese clustered to escape the racism of the dominant society were known. Don Seto's grandfather Gan Seto ran the New Look Café in High River, Alberta. Roy Mah's father had the B.K. Grocery in East Vancouver. Some jobs were fairly menial, and it may have been his classical training as a scholar and artist, or perhaps his expertise at Kung Fu, that sustained Candace Yip's grandfather Lore Neen while operating the elevator in a downtown Victoria building.

The mostly men who arrived first went to great lengths to have a family life. Gail Yip's grandfather, who had immigrated with his parents to New Westminster at the age of eight, made several trips to China before bringing the woman he had married there and their two small sons back with him to British Columbia in 1913. Joe Hop Lee wed a young woman who had been bought and brought to Canada to look after the children of a Vancouver Chinatown merchant. Arranged marriages were the rule in China, as in many parts of the world. Hayne Wai's grandmother was sixteen when, in 1914, a Hong Kong marriage broker matched her with a middle-aged merchant, Wong Wah, who had arrived in Victoria three decades earlier and now wanted to start a family. They met for the first time on her wedding day. Dan Seto's mother knew only rural China at the time she married her Canadianized husband in Hong Kong.

Arrived in Canada, these women not only raised families but worked alongside their husbands and also in other jobs bringing a bit of money into the family economy. Hayne Wai's grandmother sewed; Roy Mah's mother worked in a garment factory and peeled shrimp on the Vancouver docks. Young children helped out. Roy Mah recalled, among other tasks, translating for his father in his Vancouver store.

Whatever the time period, the family life obtained in British Columbia was closely guarded. Belinda Hung's grandmother Poh-Poh, who had earlier experienced the discrimination of South Africa, used flowers to create a beauty transcending race in her Burnaby home. The most important lesson Dan Seto took away from his grandfather was for he and his three brothers to respect each other. Being in one of the few Chinese families in town gave young Dan repeated opportunities to protect his brothers and also to represent his family's Chinese culture. Gail Yip and Hayne Wai each lovingly depict their grandparents' homes and ways of life in Vancouver, as they recall them from their early childhoods. Most revealing are the family photos forming part of each of the stories.

Parents and grandparents sometimes modeled for their members little shows of independence challenging the deference expected of them by the dominant society. Dan Seto's grandfather popped a Canadian beaver into the traditional Chinese medicine he brewed for months on end and then gave the beaver to his grandson to take to school for show-and-tell. Candace Yip's aunt Victoria was taken by her artist father Lore Neen to whitewash classical Chinese characters on Mount Douglas outside of Victoria, a feat the local newspaper speculated were local Japanese signaling to invading ships or planes. Roy Mah's father was so fed up with robberies of his grocery store that, the next time, he pulled out the machete he used to cut popsicles in half that was far longer than the knife held by the hopeful robber.

The stories are also about family mobility. Unlike the rest of Canada, the majority of the non-Aboriginal population in British Columbia has always been—and continues to be—born outside of the province. We live at a distance from our inheritance and so do not have, in Belinda Hung's words, "the security of a stable cultural identity."

Some families moved back and forth in order to survive economically and emotionally. Hayne Wai was five when he and his family arrived from Hong Kong in 1952 to live with his grandparents, ostensibly as immigrants but in reality to become a part of a family whose origins in British Columbia stretched back to 1884. In 1922 Shirley Chan's grandparents Joe and Lim Hop Lee returned to China with their ten Canadian-born children in the hopes of securing them a better life free of the racism endemic in Vancouver. The result was mixed, in part because their Canadian-born children were expected to defer to his first family left behind in China and in part because everyday life, especially for girls and women, was far more restricted than in Canada. Joe's return to Canada to make the money needed to sustain both families left his daughters especially adrift. Family memories are not necessarily happy ones. Real life doesn't always work out that way.

The stories are not so much about living between cultures as about living in two cultures. On searching out his grandfather's death in 1925 in Cranbook, Ken Yip discovered a front-page article detailing how "Chinese and whites alike" mourned Yip Chung Ben at a funeral combining Chinese freemasonry and traditional Chinese music with a Methodist sermon and the Cranbrook city band. As a treasured family photo shows, Candace Yip's mother and her siblings were enthusiastic actors in what appears to be a Chinese opera performance in Victoria in the early 1930s, but also studied Western ballet and took piano lessons. Despite being "treated like second-class citizens," Hayne Wai's uncle James enlisted in the Second World War along with a group of his contemporaries from Vancouver's Chinatown. So did Ken Yip's father, who was part of a Special Forces unit in Burma. Even though her grandmother had bound feet, Gail Yip's recollection of an early childhood Christmas dinner is much more about Canadian family life in 1950s Vancouver than about any particular culture. Returning to Canada, Shirley Chan's mother Lee Wo Soon Chan, or Mary, successfully led the opposition to a freeway cutting through Vancouver's Chinatown in the 1960s and early 1970s.

In reading about these eight families, we are each enriched, and so is the history of Canada and of British Columbia. It is through family history that we will finally begin to comprehend the extent and diversity of the contributions made by Chinese Canadians across the generations. The time is long past for Canadians to discard the arrogant assumption held in the dominant society that all others should want to aspire toward its ways of life. As these stories attest, for a century and a half the Chinese have contributed to Canada within frames of reference as rightfully part of this country's history as are those long taken for granted as the norm. These eight stories permit us to begin to understand the diversity that distinguishes Canada as a nation.

~JEAN BARMAN

Professor Emerita
University of British Columbia

Founding Board Member
Chinese Canadian Historical
Society of British Columbia

INTRODUCTION
Starting Small

I just had a dream in which I was staying at a relative's house for a family reunion. No one explicitly said so, but I knew that I wasn't allowed in the unlocked room at the top of the stairs. Yet amidst the din of everyone's excited chatter and exchanges of affection, I was drawn to the room. Even though I tried to sneak away without being noticed, I could feel my elders' eyes bearing into my back as I climbed the stairs. Interestingly, it wasn't a disapproving or warning gaze from them I experienced, but rather one of silent encouragement and curiosity about what I might discover or do.

When I opened the door, there was a slow, pronounced creak that became the only sound in the house, as it seemed the family reunion downstairs suddenly disappeared. It was just me and the room now.

The room was dripping with soft orange light (for some reason, my family dreams are always characterized by their orange glow) and dust kicked up after not having moved in decades. In fact, the room had a centuries-old mustiness about it—a humid sweetness exuding from preservation whose purpose had been long forgotten.

I crossed the room to open the window, and cold air and sounds of birds chirping rushed in. Waves of lived experiences flashed between the walls with an urgent energy, raising goose bumps all over my body, yet I was comforted by scanning the pictures on the nightstand, walls, and dresser.

I finally released the breath I had been holding since I entered the room and peeked out the door and downstairs, to find that everyone who came to the family reunion was staring up at me with enigmatic smiles. Then I woke up.

Whenever I am immersed in a project, I dream about it. I kept wondering when I was going to have my CCHS Family History Writing Workshop dream—and I believe this was it. Yet this dream is not the first I have ever had when it comes to writing down my own family stories. I've been having these dreams (and often times nightmares) for a while, but this one has been one of the more encouraging ones.

Writing family stories is a tricky, sensitive process and journey. The first issues we encountered and discussed at the beginning of our six weeks together in the workshop were where to start and how to trust one's memory. These were the two major concerns that we revisited over and over again during the six weeks and which I am sure the participants are still struggling with as they continue to write their stories.

The first question—where to start—came up even before we had our first session, as I handed out preliminary exercises to help the participants begin to think about their stories. "I have so much I want to write about." "I want to leave a legacy for my children and grandchildren." "I don't even know where to begin." I know how the task, as some have come to see it, of writing family stories is daunting, especially when the rest of your family appoints you as the "family historian," as was the case for some of the participants. There is also an inherent richness to writing these stories, and therefore, everyone wants them to be grand stories with a beginning, middle, and end. Unfortunately, this is not how life and memory work.

"Start small," I told them. "Write the small stories, small memories, and work from there. Write down your stories one memory, one snippet at a time, even if it means only writing down one sentence." The participants said they only knew bits of the past, that they didn't know the whole picture. My response: to write down what you do know. You can find out the rest later, or maybe even never, but what's important is to write down how you experience your family's past.

This is where people became uneasy. "How do I trust my memory? How do I 'make up' stories like you said? I want to write the truth, the facts." The real truth, I told them, is that you may never know the truth. In fact, in reality, you will never know the truth because the past has already been lived. Even professional historians don't really know the truth—they interpret events based on what is available to them as "evidence" of history, but sometimes even these documents are faulty. In the present, people make stuff up—they forge documents, buy other people's papers, create new identities, even come up with different birth and death dates. Years later, we hold those papers in our hands and take them as truth. We experience them as something else than what they originally were intended to be. And that was what the mission of the workshop was supposed to be: to write about our experiences, our own "truths," with the past.

Nonetheless, all this writing based on our own experiences still causes apprehension and anxiety. We worry about what other people, especially our families, will think of our versions of family lore. I encouraged the participants to speak with their families, get them involved with the process, if they felt they needed second opinions on their writings. Some of them did just that, while others shied away from getting their families involved, trusting in their own voices and memories. Only the writer can decide which level of family involvement works for himself or herself.

Yet in the end, writing is a solitary act. One sits down at the computer or with pen and paper to recreate worlds in his or her own mind, in which he or she has lived. For this reason, unless one has the incredible tenacity to keep at it because he or she finds it worthy enough, many stories are left untold and are silenced. Most people will say, "Why would anyone want to read what I write or listen to what I have to say," and generations come and go with the stories being buried and forgotten with those who passed on. This is why I have been organizing writing workshops for the past six years—because I know that everyone's stories are worthy enough, and if one puts in some effort, they will be told and remembered.

Writing workshops are a communal act, providing a supportive and encouraging environment in which people can exchange stories for feedback. Having gone through and continuing to go through the process of writing my own family stories about my Vietnamese mother and Pennsylvania Dutch father, I know all about self-doubt when it comes to writing. But sharing stories with other folks in a safe environment and hearing people say, "I know what you're talking about," is a great affirmation that what you're writing is on the right track. And the process of sharing breaks the silences that have shrouded our family stories, paying homage to the legacy of those who have worked hard and struggled to give their descendents a better life in a new country.

The six weeks spent in the CCHS Family History Writing Workshop are a beginning to providing a new look on Chinese Canadian lives and history. I would like to thank the Chinese Canadian Historical Society board for accepting my proposal to organize and facilitate this workshop. This was my first foray back into arts organizing since I moved to Vancouver from Los Angeles, and it truly has been a rewarding experience. I would also like to thank Jan Walls and the David Lam Centre for providing the space for our workshop, space being the most complicated issue when it comes to holding workshops. Finally, the eight participants in the workshop—Shirley Chan, Belinda Hung, Roy Mah, Dan Seto, Hayne Wai, Candace Yip, Gail Yip, and Ken Yip—have taught me so much about Chinese Canadian lives, experiences, and history. They bonded over six weeks of doing take-home exercises involving such activities as combing photographs, documents, and archives for previously unnoticed details; talking with family members in order to unearth memories; trying out different perspectives, tenses, and voices; and imagining themselves as "characters" in their stories. Their hard work during the revision and structuring process has paid off in the form of this inaugural CCHS publication, and for all their efforts, I thank them.

~BRANDY LIÊN WORRALL

Workshop Organizer

A Note on Transliteration of Chinese Terms

One issue that arose while we were working on these stories was how to standardize transliterations of Chinese terms. We reached the conclusion that because everyone's families had come from different regions with different dialects of Cantonese, that each person would maintain his or her own transliteration as he or she has come to know and use them, and the reader would hopefully be able to gather from context the meanings of such words. Thus, there is variance in the Romanization of the Chinese in this collection.

"Unidentified Family, c. 1910"

THE GIRL IN THE PICTURE

Shirley Chan

Identified family, 1922. This is the same picture the Vancouver Art Gallery used in its *Gum San/Gold Mountain* catalogue in 1985, incorrectly guessing the date of it as 1910. My mother is in the back row on the far right.

*A*i ya! *Here I am — looking at this 1985 Vancouver Art Gallery catalogue,* Gum San/Gold Mountain: Images of Gold Mountain 1886-1947 *— and what do I find in it but this picture of an "Unidentified Family, c. 1910," reprinted from photographer Yucho Chow's silver gelatin print, thanks to a collector named Ian Lee! Huh, what do they know? That's me, Wo Soon — some call me Mary — standing behind my dad in this picture. This project between the VAG and the Chinese Cultural Centre is supposed to represent a new level of cooperation between the Chinese community and mainstream Vancouver. It would be great if our city's history of discrimination is really over through such a simple act of validating with these images the roles that Chinese people have played in building this city from its earliest days. We Chinese have been here for over a 100 years, with my own grandfather arriving in 1879 for the gold rush! He ended up staying to help build the railroad when he didn't strike it rich.*

Tseh! Why they didn't try harder to identify this "unidentified family"? It's not like there were many such families. After all, I'm a founding member of the Chinese Cultural Centre and an active member of its Women's Committee, but did anyone ask me to look over the photos collected and selected for exhibition? No, of course not! Why do those who speak good English because they were lucky enough to be educated here forget that those of us who weren't as lucky might have something valuable to contribute? This very photograph hangs on my living room wall — it's the oldest one from my family collection.

Let's see. . .the Vancouver Art Gallery guessed 1910, but it was actually 1922 when Dad arranged for us to have this picture taken behind our house on Slocan Street. That's where all ten of us were born. We look rather nice in this photo, but it was quite a scramble to find matching socks and shoes and presentable clothes for everyone. But then, we didn't do this just for fun, even though we were so excited to have our picture taken for the first time. No, it was because Dad had plans to take us back to China to live. The print would be cut up into individual headshots for our passports.

My dad, Joe Lee, looks handsome and proud with a son on his lap and the rest of his family arranged around him. My mom, Lim Hop Lee, manages, incredibly, to look serene and unruffled with the baby on her lap. With ten Canadian-born children ranging in age from eleven years to two months, the only quiet moment of the day was when we held still for our picture.

I look a little faded from over-exposure standing on a bench in the back row behind Dad with the sun in my eyes. My big brother George (No. 3 brother) and my younger sister Lana (No. 4 sister) are standing to my right. George was already tall and Lana, who is standing behind Mom, looks almost the same height as me even though she's a year younger. She's the only one with a smile, but then Lana's always smiling.

Big Sister No. 2 is seated beside Mom with Lily (No. 5 sister) standing to her right resting an elbow on her shoulder. On the far right is Robert (No. 4 brother) looking cocky as ever with his elbow propped on the hedge. Sitting in the chair is Yim (No. 7 sister) with No. 6 sister standing in front. They are dressed like boys because Dad was told he could sell birth certificates and citizenship papers for boys, but that no one would pay for documents for girls. Lucky for me, I was too old to pass for a boy.

○ ○ ○

In 1922, Joe and Lim Hop Lee took their Canadian-born family back to China by freighter. That was just one year before the Chinese Exclusion Act was passed. The family would be able to return to Canada during this black period in Canadian history if they were able to prove their Canadian citizenship. Wo Soon was seven years old (eight, if you count the Chinese way) and the third daughter fathered by Joe. She remembers Mrs. Barclay next door as a friend coming to the door with a tray saying: "Soon, you give these cookies to your mom for me. I made them myself, and there's too many for us." Mrs. Barclay was such a true friend that she became a regular visitor when Lim Hop Lee came back to Canada to live in 1950. But Mrs. Barclay was an exception.

Most of the time, the Lee family experienced racism when they ventured into town or even just at school. The other children would taunt, "Look out! Chinky, chinky Chinaman! Stinky, stinky Chinaman!" while snatching the apple from their hand to throw on the ground, shoving them into the mud, and ganging up on them if they were alone or out-numbered. If Mrs. Barclay saw them, she would intervene, "You boys stop that right now, or I'm telling your mother!" and they would look sheepish and stop harassing the kids.

Although Joe worked hard to keep his family fed, it wasn't easy. Depending on the season, he worked as a houseboy, chopped wood, and sold fruit and vegetables from his orchard and garden. His wife was too busy with the children to help with the farming. When Soon was old enough to help, he put her to work when he had to go to town. "Soon, you be a good girl and pull up all the weeds," he said, pointing to his garden, "and I'll bring you a treat when I come home."

Soon worked in the hot sun. She smelled the rich dirt as she pulled and dug at the little green shoots. She was careful to dig up *all* the plants, thinking the whole time of the reward she would get when her dad returned. But to her surprise, when he took one look at the garden, he screamed, "You stupid girl! I'm going to kill you! Soon! Where are you?" as Soon ran to her mother, bewildered at his rage.

Lim Hop came out to see what all the fuss was about, chiding Joe, "What's wrong? You're scaring the children! Soon worked hard all afternoon for you."

"Stupid girl pulled up all the vegetable seedlings along with the weeds!" he shouted.

Sure enough, there wasn't a single plant left, neither weed nor vegetable seedling. Soon had diligently pulled up every single one. "Well," Lim Hop shrugged, "you should have given her better instructions. She's only six years old. You can't blame her for your mistake." She led Soon by the hand into the kitchen where she washed away the dirt and tears, earning a big smile and hug when she gave her hardworking daughter the sweet preserved plums her dad brought home from Chinatown.

There were nights when the children would awaken to pungent smells wafting up from the kitchen where their dad was cooking "medicine." They would whine, "Mommy, what's that smell? I'm hot! Can I have a drink of water?" Lim Hop would wipe their brows and wake the older children to help with the younger ones. What the children didn't know was that their dad was preparing perfumy, sticky opium to supplement the family income. When Joe decided to take the family back to China, he reasoned, "It will be easier to feed them all there because the Canadian dollar goes a long way in China." He added, "It will also get the children away from the racism."

The trip in that freighter was a blur. Lim Hop and most of the children were so sick from the tossing that they couldn't keep anything down. Only Yim seemed to have inherited Joe's sea legs and was one of the few besides the crew who had any appetite. Weak from vomiting and barely able to keep down water, they nearly died from dehydration. "Ma, I feel sick! Help me!" cried each child, but Lim Hop, limp from motion sickness, was far from being able to help. It fell on Joe and three-year-old Yim to try and make them more comfortable. The smell of vomit pervaded the air, making it worse for Lim Hop to try to nurse the baby because she couldn't keep anything down to nourish even herself.

When they arrived in China, they met some of their Chinese relatives, exchanging hugs and red envelopes of money. Everyone opened presents, like the fine writing paper from Gold Mountain, and celebrated the family reunification with a big meal. They also set off firecrackers to scare away the evil spirits.

Joe had a first wife with three children—two boys and a girl—which explained why the Canadian-born family started with Sister No. 2 and Brother No. 3. The kids got along fine, and George, Soon and Bob grew fond of Louie (Big Brother No. 2). "Come on, I'll show you the pond where we can catch frogs and go fishing!" he offered excitedly.

Finding themselves in this village after being in Vancouver all their lives was a big shock. On top of that, the villagers made them feel like outcasts. "Why do they call us names? We're Chinese too, so why don't they like us?" they asked their mother.

"Shhh. It's because you were born in Canada, and they've

never been outside this village," she explained. "Try to talk and act like them, and they will forget that you weren't born here." But she often had to wipe away a tear or soothe hurt feelings. Fortunately, the older children like George and Soon seemed to tough it out quite well. In fact, on more than one occasion, she had to caution them not to fight back as it would lead to more problems.

Following their mother's advice, the children quickly learned not to speak English except among themselves and even then always out of earshot of other villagers who took pleasure in tormenting them with pejorative nicknames like "overseas Chinese" or worse "ghost sister" and "ghost boy." Before long, they adapted to Chinese language and ways in an effort to put an end to this new type of discrimination. But the fact that Joe sent all his children to school didn't help matters.

"It's the Canadian way, the way of the future," he said, "to send both my sons and daughters to school. In Canada, girls go to school." However, the villagers didn't share his ideas, and the girls were taunted mercilessly when walking through the village to and from school. "Useless Gold Mountain family—educate your daughters, and they will kill their husbands," they chanted.

Joe was too far away to hear any of this as he had sailed back to Gold Mountain soon after getting his family settled in China. He sent remittances regularly, but he didn't return for years.

It wasn't easy growing up in China. There were many unfair rules for girls! "Why can't I climb trees and skip or run like we did in Vancouver?" demanded Soon, eyes blazing and arms akimbo. "I don't care what those villagers think. It's not fair!" It was fortunate for Soon, who had her own ideas, that her dad took pride in being a modern man who believed in educating his daughters, or she could have ended up like those villagers whose ignorance she despised. Yet for the most part, she and her siblings learned to conform. That is, until she ran headlong into her father's wishes. She was just fifteen when asked to put on some new clothes and accompany her older sister through the village.

A "wealthy" Gold Mountain merchant had returned to China to choose a second wife or concubine to bear him sons. He knew Joe had several Canadian-born daughters and arranged to see his eldest. Unexpectedly, the man picked Soon instead of her sister because she was stronger and livelier—the better to bear sons. When Soon heard that her dad had promised to marry her to this old man, she flatly refused, "No way I'm marrying anybody right now and certainly not some old man from Gum San whom I never met!" No matter what Lim Hop said, Soon refused to comply.

Joe lost face, had to return the bride wealth, and was furious. His letter was scathing, "It is obvious that you have not succeeded in raising obedient children," he wrote to his wife, "therefore, I am not sending any more money until your children learn how to behave properly and show filial piety." He stopped sending remittances for months, and Lim Hop had to pawn her jewellery to buy food, but Soon was never repentant. She was her father's daughter—and a strong will coupled with education had produced a forceful personality.

"I will choose my own husband," Soon declared, and it came to pass. She met Walter (Wah Ko), who was her teacher although he was just a year older. Handsome and intelligent, Walter wrote beautiful characters and poetry with firm brush strokes! His singing voice was a marvel—a clear tenor that carried across the schoolyard. "I adore going to his class, and he's patient when I ask questions," Soon gushed to her sisters. After she graduated and also started teaching, Soon and Walter chummed with the same group of friends. One summer day, she discovered that all the guys could swim but none of the gals could, so in her usual fashion she accepted the challenge of trying to swim—gasping and splashing in the refreshing pond by the waterfall.

"Don't let the villagers know or your reputation will be ruined! Nice girls don't strip off most of their clothes to splash around in the water when men are around," her girlfriends teased.

When Soon came home one day with her braid cut off, her mom was upset but refrained from scolding. With tightly pursed lips, she gave her a red ribbon to wear in her hair to ward off the evil spirits. She was afraid that her high-spirited daughter would be arrested, as were many teachers, for being a communist.

"Today, I told Mom that Walter and I want to marry," Soon reported to her sisters.

"What did she say?" they clamoured. "What do you think will happen? Will you marry Walter even if Dad says no?"

"I told Mom that we are going to marry and that we weren't asking permission but would like their blessing. She said she would break it to Dad in her next letter and tell him that she approves. I think she is happy because her own marriage was arranged between Dad and the family that had bought her and brought her to Canada to look after their children and help with chores — the merchant family that owned Gim Lee Yuen Company in Chinatown."

After their wedding in 1936, the newlyweds were sent to different villages to teach. They would miss each other and their families, but they believed in the importance of their work.

"We have decided to join the government's new literacy program," she announced to her family. "I will teach the children in this rural community and show them how they can go home to teach their parents, grandparents and older siblings who stay behind to help at home or on the farm." She sewed a few cotton *cheong-sam*, packed a small bag and bid her husband goodbye.

Passionate about her role as teacher, Soon developed a reputation for telling wonderful stories to her classes. "Listen, boys and girls," she promised, "I will tell you a story tomorrow if the whole class gets 100% on dictation." So in the classroom as in their homes, the older and brighter children eagerly helped the younger and slower ones. When they all got perfect scores, she would weave a story filled with children and animals and magic.

"It really warms my heart to see how hard the children try and how hungry they are to learn. Education is opening opportunities and new worlds to these children which they didn't know existed. Being a teacher is the best job in the world," wrote Soon, the proud young teacher, to her new husband far away.

My father, 1955.

My mother, 1948.

This picture is of me and my parents in 1949. I am two years old here, and my father just arrived from China. This is our first family picture.

Author's Note

I was born at St. Paul's Hospital in Vancouver three months after my mother, Lee Wo Soon Chan, returned to Canada in 1947. From her I learned to knock on neighbours' doors to organize the community. We succeeded in stopping the demolition of our home and the Strathcona neighbourhood by the construction of a freeway through Chinatown in the late 1960s and early 1970s.

I took this workshop hoping to learn how to write and do the necessary research to authenticate the story of my mother's life. With most of that generation already passed away, I have to rely on memories of stories told to me and on siblings and cousins. Nevertheless, I found the experience of learning and sharing so enriching that I am encouraged to continue. I want to leave my children a legacy so they appreciate how, courtesy of their grandmother, we are able to enjoy the freedom and privileges of living in Canada.

This story centres around my mother, whose family portrait appears in a Vancouver Art Gallery exhibit and catalogue unbeknownst to her. We begin in Vancouver where the children were born and the photograph was taken; and cross the Pacific to a village in southern China where they grew up. My mother was always breaking traditions, including making a love match when she married my father.

Other people I would like to write about are my grandfather, who worked on the railroad; my grandmother, who was sold to a merchant family and came to Canada as a servant; and members of my generation.

This workshop taught me to include the five senses and to bring my family members to life with dialogue and structure. Photographs were used to serve as memory aids, and the importance of context, history and description was stressed. I still need to find documents that will help me anchor my story.

The greatest value of the workshop is getting tips on how to get started and to put pen to paper or fingers to keyboard. Thank you, Brandy!

~Shirley Chan

紫禁城

The Forbidden Palace

Belinda Hung

My inheritance from the past — my family history and Chinese cultural ancestry — has often felt like the Forbidden Palace, the ancient dwelling for Chinese emperors and untold priceless treasures. The entrance into this vast complex, thought to be located under the centre of heaven, was prohibited to all but the members of the imperial family and their guests. Likewise, I have felt barred, by language and spectres of the past, from a sense of home and the security of a stable cultural identity.

Though I was born in Canada, I have struggled with a sense of belonging. While growing up, well intentioned people have questioned me as to where I'm from. On the other hand, I don't speak, read or write Chinese. So where is "home"?

The journey of examining the past and voicing my own narrative has been helpful in coming home to myself where I no longer allow others to define who I am or what it means to be Chinese. Exploring this Forbidden Palace of the past has been a process of passing through its many gates and over its countless thresholds, and finally to making claim to its very centre and throne.

紫 禁 城

The Meridian Gate looms large before me. I pass through and enter the grand city complex of the Forbidden Palace to explore a few of its many thousands of rooms. Here is where I find the hidden treasures of the past that bring me to myself and home.

紫 禁 城

SEEDING

The people in our lives often become like titles of a book that we've never read. I pick one up in my mind, *Grandfather — Kong*, and am overwhelmed by a whole lifetime and wealth of experience of which I would have never guessed. To find those missing pages of our ancestry is both the challenge and the reward, for in recovering the lives of our elders, we also somehow discover ourselves through their stories. Recording those histories as they've touched us is the journey. Where will it take us?

紫 禁 城

As a newborn, I first met my maternal grandfather when he was sixty. He was born in China in 1913 (October 7, we believe, though we know it isn't the exact date), and I was born in 1973 in Canada. In those sixty years before my birth, he went from Lancaster, China to Krugesdorp, South Africa to Burnaby, Canada. His life has spanned three continents, and this detail alone invokes untold adventures.

Those adventures came roaring to life for me as a child when it slipped out of my mother's mouth one day that my grandfather had been kidnapped by bandits as a boy. Magic and excitement suddenly swirled about my family and seeded a hungry curiosity —what was the hidden story?

紫 禁 城

Leong Gew Sar (Lancaster Village), Guangdong Province, China, Summer 1926.

The night is dark and fragrant. I shuffle about near the inside of the village gate, listening to the elders chatting, their bits of conversation floating through the air like filaments of silk.

I wonder if what the school principal said today is true. Kidnappings? He told us we could go home to our villages today because of the rumours that have been circulating. . .and then after dinner, Mama told me not to stay out too late tonight! But in any case, I want to go back to Lok Tong Hui tomorrow for hui jrat, *market day! I'll tell Mama I have to pick up my belongings from the boarding school…I left my stuff there deliberately today just so I'd have an excuse to go out tomorrow!*

Earlier this evening, I heard Ah Terng say that he saw some strange people in the mulberry orchards just outside the village gate. I wonder if they're there…maybe I can see them, but it's so dark!

What's that? There are noises coming from outside the gate! The others hear it too and peer out into the blackness. Maybe the rumours are true!

Shouts: "What do you want?! What are you doing here?!"

All of a sudden, flashlights shine out, and gunshots rip through the air as the village gate bursts open!

Adrenaline pumping, everyone runs. To the river! There's Ah Hung

13

swimming already. What's happening? I jump into the water, but for some reason I cling to the banks, lost. I am captured.

紫 禁 城

My grandfather was kept a prisoner for 100 days while his family and village collected the 3,000 pieces of silver that his kidnappers demanded for his return. His village was raided because the bandits knew that many of the families living there had relatives in *Gum Saan* (South Africa) and thus were wealthy enough to meet their ransom demands.

When he was finally released, his legs were so weak that he could barely walk, so he *zhung zhung ha*, stumbled along like a newborn calf, venturing into a new chapter in his life. For within a year, my grandfather was living in South Africa. His family, fearful of the dangers in China and badly shaken by the kidnapping, believed South Africa would provide a better life.

Now, my grandfather, at a spry ninety-two, lives in Burnaby. Such are the twistings of life. He has been in Canada for over thirty-seven years.

Grandfather — Kong: I summon his image to mind, he is laughing, his eyes twinkling with mischief and mirth. I know I've only just scratched the surface. . .so many more pages in this book.

紫 禁 城

FLOWERING

Flowers. There are always flowers. Over the years, birthdays, weddings, graduations and anniversaries in my mother's family have all been marked with a beautiful touch — a flower arrangement made by my grandmother.

When I used to get sick as a child, my grandmother, Poh-Poh, would always send me a bunny rabbit made from a large white mum, with pipe cleaner eyes, satin wire ears and finished off with a very smart-looking perfectly formed blue bow at his neck. Sadly, I knew I had grown up when my little long-eared friend no longer appeared when I got sick.

I've seen Poh-Poh work with flowers from time to time. As

a youngster, I would watch in wonderment. She would take the sharp knife and cut each stem at an angle, instinctively knowing the right length for each one to make a balanced arrangement. She worked with such care, grace and fluidity amongst the symphony of blooms. Each petal, each budding curlicue had its proper place.

She takes the same precision with most everything else. My mother remarked to me with exasperation how one evening after our family Sunday dinner had wrapped up, Poh-Poh would not rest until she had rearranged her cupboards back into the proper order! Someone in the family didn't put away the washed cups and plates into the right place. . .oops!

I think my grandmother must have always been this way — careful and caring in every action. Looking at old photos of my mother's family back in "S.A." (South Africa), I note the perfect press to their dresses, crisp and white, the neat finish to their hair, bows tied in place, and the slight angle of the feet in order to pose for the camera. She sewed all of her children's clothing herself.

I have never been to South Africa, but I imagine it as a supremely beautiful country, covered with exotic blooms, bursting with life and colour. It should have been a place to flourish and grow. But no — in my grandfather's words: "South Africa denies you if you are not White. They call it White. They classify you as Black, Asian, White, Coloured. They divide everyone and you carry a book telling your class." The prison bars of race dictated where you could live, whom you could marry, where your children could go to school. Apartheid means apartness — enforced separation.

I see my Poh-Poh as a mother of five, living in apartheid South Africa. I pull bits of stories together to try and read the larger story.

Grandmother — Poh-Poh: careful and caring. She told me once how she would have to wipe the spit off her son's forehead when he came home. Feces left at the front entrance to their store had to be washed away some mornings. My grandmother, asking permission for her daughters to attend the white Catholic school, is told by the Head Mother to make sure that her children don't draw undue attention to themselves.

Careful and caring. My grandmother watched the racial tensions in South Africa grow worse and wanted her children to be safe. In 1964, she embarked on an expedition to find the best place for her family to thrive. New York, Montreal. . .she chose Vancouver.

I see my grandmother now, at her home in Burnaby, where she has lived for almost forty years. She is carefully arranging yellow daisies into a basket for her great-granddaughter's first birthday party. We go to the party. The flowers make a sunny spot on the table. Holly, the birthday girl, is full of smiles, sitting in front of her cake. Her Nana and Granddad look on from one side, and Tai-Poh and Tai-Kong (my Poh-Poh and Kong) watch from the other.

Grandmother—Poh-Poh: careful and caring. The blooms are a mass of different colours all in one arrangement—no separation. She is gentle with the stems, but I can see the strength of her still. Her vision comes alive beneath her hands. It is a beautiful flowering.

紫 禁 城

GERMINATING

When I lived in my family's home in Burnaby, there was a photo on the wall of our crammed basement rec room that hung in the background all those years—and which was the one visual link to my father's past. I never examined the photo this closely before, but now that I am looking at a copy of it, I can say that there were actually two photos in the frame—the one on the right-side is a close-up shot of my paternal grandfather in his air force uniform taken in Shanghai at Wou Kong Studio (date unknown); to the left, there is a photo of him and a fellow comrade. They are wearing identical uniforms and hats, with winged insignia affixed to their tunics, and are standing in front of an old-fashioned biplane—an airplane that has two wings, one above the other. They look young and vibrant and yes, even heroic. My grandfather is smiling, and he has his arm around his buddy. They must have just graduated from flight school because there are tied scrolls in their hands.

Apparently, my grandfather was one of the first to graduate as a pilot in China, or so I remember hearing. When WWII broke out, he returned to China from Hong Kong to fight for his country. For this show of patriotism, someone once said that if we visited China and announced who our grandfather was, that the government would give us a parade. Exaggeration, mystique and

16

adventure always seem to waft about him. "That's my father!" my father would puff out proudly, pointing at the photos. My mother told me last week that the close-up shot of my grandfather is now displayed on a shelf in my father's apartment, paired with a photo of his childhood family.

紫 禁 城

I never knew my grandfather since he died in 1951 when my father was only a boy. He passed away before the age of fifty, from high blood pressure like his father before him. Drinking, smoking and gambling were the causes of his early death, according to my father and uncle. However, they still speak of him in glowing, almost mythical terms, like a hero—as young boys who idealize their fathers often do. My grandmother, Sally, remembers him in the same way. She never remarried after her husband's death.

Apart from these few details, however, my father's family history is shrouded in mystery. I haven't spoken to my father for almost twelve years, and the twenty years that we lived in the same household, I never felt free to ask him questions about his past.

Even the photos I have of my father and his family were gained surreptitiously. As he was preparing to move out of the family home in 2001, my mother smuggled some of his photo albums that had lain hidden in the back of his closet and colour-copied them for me.

Why the secrecy? I'm not sure. If asked, I believe he would try to answer my questions to the best of his ability. But somehow my relationship with my father is so damaged that I have chosen to end communication with him.

So those photos I received from my mother were like a beautiful small window onto a time I never knew. I saw my father as a blameless young boy—one who had lost his own father, the "hero pilot," at the age of thirteen and who was then raised by his paranoid schizophrenic mother. She went undiagnosed with the illness until she immigrated to Canada in the 1970s.

紫 禁 城

I pull out one of the colour-copied pictures from my father's childhood—my favourite photograph of him. It's a group shot of twenty-five of my relatives, probably a family reunion dinner at a restaurant in Shanghai around 1947. There, on the left-side of the picture, in a trio is my grandfather, smiling, with a cigarette in his hand, holding onto my aunt who is perched on top of a chair beside my father. My other aunt is standing with a sour expression on her face on the far right of the frame next to her seated brother (my uncle), who is the only one not facing the camera. My grandmother, with a Mona Lisa smile on her face, stands in the very corner of the room, her face just visible, wedged between her sisters. I don't recognize anyone else, but my grandmother came from a family of twelve, so the other adults in the photo are probably her siblings. It also dawns on me that the elderly woman seated at the centre of the shot could possibly be my great-grandmother.

I shift to examine my father in the photo. I pull myself upwards to peer through the beautiful small window where I can look upon that young boy. He is about nine years old, wearing a suit jacket and tie and leaning on a chair with a big grin on his face. Eyes alight, he seems barely able to contain his enthusiasm at the new *Don Winslow* comic book that he is clutching and which he proudly displays for the camera. I imagine him running around excitedly with the comic book in hand. My uncle, at the other end of the table, is also holding up his comic book, *The Lone Ranger*.

Don Winslow — I'm not familiar with that comic book character. Searching online, I find that Don Winslow was once a major comic strip and comic book character in the 1930s and 1940s. Originally created as propaganda to recruit more men into the navy, the hero, Don Winslow, WWI vet, was a naval intelligence agent assigned to handle major threats to world peace, including combating his arch-nemesis, the Scorpion and his evil organization, Scorpia! The comic book ended in 1955, with Don Winslow fading into obscurity.

I don't know how my father got this American comic book, which I presume he was able to read since my grandmother, raised in the Philippines, spoke and even taught English. Maybe my grandfather picked up the comic book from his travels. I know my grandmother used to order gloves and other expensive items from American catalogues. They must have been quite well off. I wonder what they did for money when my grandfather died just four years later.

Grandfather — the Hero died in 1951 and faded into the past, into a photograph that now sits in my father's apartment.

紫　禁　城

Father—Grandfather. There are missing pages in these books that I
may never find, but the pages I do have I've tried to piece together.
Looking at the group photo, I know that that young jubilant boy is
still somewhere in my father. I imagine him looking with fondness
at the photograph of his own father in uniform. His grief for the
father he lost matches my own.

紫　禁　城

*I enter the Hall of Supreme Harmony and ascend the steps leading to the
intricately carved golden throne that is covered with coiling dragons. I smooth
my hand over the yellow silk cushion. I am no longer an outsider. Here is
the centre, and here is my home.*

紫　禁　城

My grandfather's pictures as a pilot, c. 1925.

Photographs courtesy of author.

The picture of my father's family when he was a boy in
Shanghai, c. 1947. My grandfather is in the back row on the
left, and my father is in the middle row, second from the left,
holding his *Don Winslow* comic book.

I was born in Burnaby, B.C. in 1973 and am a first-generation Canadian. Though my roots eventually trace back to two provinces in southern China—Fujian on my father's side and Guangdong on my mother's—there are many twisting branches feeding into my family history that reflect the wide-ranging diversity of the Chinese diaspora.

My mother was born and raised in Krugesdorp, South Africa, as was her mother before her. My father was born in Hong Kong, but spent his youth in Calcutta and Shanghai. His father was also born in Hong Kong, while my paternal grandmother grew up in the Philippines. I have relatives scattered all over the world, including Singapore, England, South Africa, China, the United States, and across Canada.

I am interested in the way that the lives of our ancestors, whether that past is known or not, affects and shapes the current generation. I am especially drawn to those experiences relegated to the shadows, the family's taboos and secrets, that cry out for healing.

I approached this workshop with trepidation. It is not easy to give voice to parts of our family history that are painful and silenced. As such, the writing process has been both challenging and therapeutic for me. To those of you in a similar situation, a word of encouragement: I have thus far found that most of the "blocks" have been internally resolved, i.e., I have not so much been confronted with external resistance to my questions about the past but rather the issue has been: am I willing to ask those questions, am I ready to hear the answers, and am I prepared to write about them openly?

Thank you to CCHS, my fellow workshop participants, and Brandy Liên Worrall for the experience! It has been a pleasure to read the stories of the other writers and behold the beautiful diversity of voices that this forum has brought forth. Through Brandy's efforts, we have each gotten our "writing legs" beneath us. We have moved through exercises, drafts, feedback, editing, and finally to publication in six short weeks!

Lastly, my love goes out to my family. I have endeavoured to write about my experience of our shared history with a true and open heart.

~Belinda Hung

B.K. Grocery

Roy Mah

The front of my father's store, 1968.

My father in his store, B.K. Grocery, December 1985.

In *Saving Private Ryan*, a squad of eight soldiers goes behind enemy lines to find Private James Ryan to escort him home. The General orders the mission necessary because Ryan's three brothers were already killed in combat. Faced with impossible odds, the soldiers question their orders, and in the end six out of eight soldiers pay the ultimate sacrifice. As the captain lies dying, he whispers into Private Ryan's ear, "Earn this. Earn it." Years later, James Ryan brings his family to the captain's grave, where James confesses to the headstone, "I've tried to live my life the best I could. I hope that was enough. I hope that at least in your eyes, I've earned what all of you have done for me."

For me, the theme of the movie hits home. My parents also made tremendous sacrifices for their children. When my parents made the decision to leave China, the communists were becoming the ruling party, and all business owners were deemed to be enemies of the state. Because my parents owned a business, they would be subjected to torture or even death. So they escaped from China to Hong Kong, leaving behind all their worldly possessions, including their house and store. Once in Canada, my parents continued to struggle in their new business, facing a society trying to take advantage of their vulnerabilities.

O   O   O

The store feels antiquated in a location surrounded by newly built single-family homes. Though the banner sign is showing its age with bits of chipped-away paint, the building has an old-age appeal. You notice the steep roof, two top rounded windows, and the large front display window looking out onto the street. As you approach the corner of 34th Avenue and Nanaimo Street, you are struck by the two-storey red brick structure. Records suggest that a bricklayer named Harry Bridge of 5131 Highgate Street in South Vancouver probably built it in 1917-1918. It became a grocery store in 1920, and the owner's initials are proudly displayed in the "BK Grocery" sign, which divides the upper living quarters from the storefront below.

The store window, plastered with cigarette posters and the familiar red plastic Cola-Cola characters, occupies the width of the front. Facing Nanaimo Street is a huge blue square sign displaying the Player's cigarette symbol — sign rental being another source of revenue for the store.

An outside staircase leads to the upper floor, and just behind the staircase is a large open carport. Right beside the staircase is a small, un-insulated shed used as storage for goods. The area is very residential, and there is an elementary school close by. For neighborhood convenience, the store opens at 8 A.M. and closes at 9 P.M. Children mingle in front of the store, eating the popsicles and chips they just bought. A teenage girl is sweeping the sidewalk and picking up the scattered candy wrappers.

As you push the green door into the store, a bell announces your entrance. You immediately notice that the space feels crammed. Wooden shelves and coolers are spread out in the tiny room. To the left of the door are bags of potatoes stacked one on top of the other. The aisle is wide enough for only one person. You face shelves of canned beans, cereal boxes, candy in plastic bags. A stout smiling Asian man behind the milk fridge that does double duty as the service counter greets you with "Good morning." The owner speaks little English but appears to grasp the business side of running the store.

A manual cash register is to the left, and a heavy gold-coloured scale is to the right of the counter. On the counter is a small sloping rack displaying rows of Lifesavers and Wrigleys gum. A wire shelving unit containing bags of potato chips sits in front of the scale. Who can resist the garlic shoestring potato chips clipped onto the side? A black high wooden stool relieves the constant strain of standing.

You have to ask for cigarettes behind the counter, located there because cigarettes are the most profitable item in the store. Players, Rothman's, Export A's and Sportsman are prominently displayed. Above these are Old Port, White Owl, and Marguerite cigars, including pouches of pipe tobacco. The next row displays Crackerjacks, five-cent Rainbows, fifteen-cent Fundips, and yellow bubble gum pouches.

You pick up a loaf of bread, fruit, and a bag of buns from the center wooden shelving console. On the top centre console are packages of Twinkies and Ding Dongs, and cookies, marshmallows, flour, and sugar take up the rest of the space. The red Coke cooler to the right is inviting, and you want nothing more than to open a fresh bottle. You remove the bottle cap and add it to the collection in the removable bin below. Next to the Coke cooler is a blue postal stamp dispenser where you insert change, pull one of the levers downward, and retrieve the stamps. A green portable radio against the wall is playing soft music. You watch as a customer requesting paper towels from one of the top shelves waits. The owner uses a "claw," a wooden stick with steel handles that when compressed, rubberized prongs at the top close to grab the products.

24

Just behind the store is the kitchen. The smell of salted fish wafts through the opening, and when you peek in, you can see a small woman cooking supper. A Coca-Cola radio sits on top of the fridge. A young boy with a mischievous smile leans against the fridge, and ever so slightly jerks the fridge with his palm and the radio shuts off. You can hear sounds of children playing on the upper level. The woman sees you peeking in curiously and waves you through. She takes you upstairs, where there are three very small bedrooms, a living room and a bathroom. The northeast bedroom has funky green walls and a night table separating the two beds. At the end of one bed sits a dresser and a red folding mahjong table serving as a desk at the foot of the other bed. A pot of boiling water sits in the boys' bedroom. Two girls share the other bedroom. A very young boy is singing what sounds like "Gee Mau Woo" in the girls' room. Close by is a big hardcover book, Reader's Digest Treasury. The upper level is alive with youthful activity while the parents work downstairs.

○ ○ ○

In the beginning Dad had a difficult time with his lack of English as he carried out the daily business and learned the grocery items. During the day, Mom worked at the Aero Garment Factory or peeled shrimp at the docks. I spent whatever little time I had between school and work to translate for him. The odd customer would also try to teach Dad some phrases, greetings, or names of items. Some of the more humourous, and probably embarrassing, incidents involved female customers attempting to purchase feminine hygiene products.

As we did our homework upstairs, we would run downstairs whenever we heard the doorbell ring nonstop because we knew Dad would be overwhelmed with customers. At other times, one of us accompanied him to either H. Y. Louie or Malkins wholesalers to replenish stock. Once back, the hundred-pound potato bags were split and measured out on the large scale into five- and ten-pound bags. Stacking the chips was quite a chore because the old ones had to be taken to the front and lined up row-by-row and inserted between two stacks, pyramid-style. Similarly, canned goods were stamped with a rotary price marker and placed with labels facing customers.

In the summer, we were busy packing empty pop bottles into cardboard cartons, filling the pop machine, and storing the empties in the storage hut. When Weston's (baker for Sunbeam breads) went on strike, we had to make a special trip to pick up bread. For all that trouble, we only needed to pick up a tray of bread, about two dozen loaves. Each day we eagerly looked for the delivery of fresh glazed or long john donuts. When not busy, we dusted the top of cans and stacked milk under the counter cooler. At closing time, the floor had to be swept.

When the work was done, we went outside and played in our own small "playground," an odd-shaped concrete slab whose purpose no one knew. The concrete slab was "home" whenever we played hide-and-go-seek with the neighbourhood kids. Up against the white picket fence separating our yard with our neighbour's, my brother burned ants with his magnifying glass—a reddish brown circular one that neatly rotated into a plastic sleeve—and killed slugs with salt.

The biggest troubles we encountered were the robberies. The girls never worked alone; one of the brothers was always there. A male presence offered a sense of security, or so we believed.

One day Mom, Dad, and young James were visiting relatives. On their return James ran through the front door and called out Jack's name, but there was no response. James thought my brother was going to pop out of nowhere and scare him. As they made their way past the counter and into the kitchen, Jack and Kathy were sitting on the green floor mat. Jack immediately cried out that they were just robbed. It was a matter of minutes until the police arrived after the telephone call. Jack had to tell the same story over and over to different officers. As his story went, the robbers were taller than he was, one had deep-set eyes, and they were holding probably a pellet gun as the hole was small. They took the cash from the register and a few cartons of cigarettes. A couple of days later, a small article appeared in the *Vancouver Sun* regarding the robbery. So many customers expressed their concern and anger. What a community we lived in!

Another robbery attempt was foiled when the robber pulled out a knife demanding money. Enraged, Dad pulled out a long and dull machete (used to cut popsicles in half) and challenged him. It was the classic *Crocodile Dundee* scene: "That's a knife?! Now this is a knife!" Sure enough, the robber fled. Minutes later, the police were snickering at Dad's story. All these incidents happened despite the fact that a detective lived just across the street.

26

From their penniless arrival in Canada, to their learning the ropes of owning a Western business and defending themselves, working for nearly twenty years without so much as a vacation, my parents are at the same time typical of Chinese immigrant parents yet exceptional in what they sacrificed for their children. I would like to say to them, "I've tried to live my life the best I could. I hope that was enough. I hope that at least in your eyes, I've earned what both of you have done for me."

My parents in front of their store, 1985.

Photograph courtesy of Kathy Arnsdorf.

Author's Note

Time sure goes by fast. It seems like only yesterday that a twelve-year-old boy came to Canada with his family. Since that time, I have been educated at UBC and worked as a professional engineer for over thirty years. Our challenge to assimilate in a new country was not new, but the time period was unique. Nowadays, whenever our family gathers around the kitchen table and talks about the old times, my two sons, daughter, nieces and nephews are very intrigued but do not appear to grasp the sacrifices the older generation had to endure. They not only want to know how but also why we immigrated. Therefore, I am hoping that by writing my family history, I can leave a legacy for future generations to appreciate the struggles our parents experienced by their decision to come to Canada.

This story, "B.K. Grocery," is a collaborative effort among myself and my siblings, whose memories are much better than mine, especially my brother, James. They have supplied most of the minute details in the story. My sister, Kathy, provided the accompanying photographs, and her collection on the earlier times is now the envy of the family.

For an engineer, writing is not my forte. This workshop has shown me that Chinese family history is integral to Canadian culture. Brandy Liên Worrall, our facilitator, demonstrated the various techniques used to bring to life these family stories. Group critique was also invaluable. A bonus was meeting people who have similar desires to write their own unique and interesting stories. For me, the single biggest obstacle in writing family history is wondering where to begin. I learned that it really doesn't matter where or when to start, as long as you start to write. Thanks to the workshop, my inertia to write has been broken. The workshop gave us all the courage to write.

~Roy Mah

The Beaver Tale and Other Stories

Dan Seto

My grandfather was a man of few words. But when my brothers Hopland, Lewis, Hopman, and I were young, he gave one piece of advice to us that we have never forgotten. "*Gee gen yu, henn ai- whah hai,*" he would say in the Toisan dialect, which is spoken in southern China.

At first, we didn't know what he meant, but eventually, I learned that he was telling us, "The most important thing for brothers is to respect each other." My mother would also say this phrase to us whenever we boys would get into a fight.

"Remember what your grandfather said about respecting each other," she added, as we pounded each other.

My grandfather was the youngest of three brothers. I wondered if my grandfather respected his brothers. He certainly never talked about them.

We lived in a small town called High River, Alberta, just south of Calgary. It was a predominantly farming and ranching community. My grandfather operated a restaurant called the New Look Café. We lived above the restaurant, so we would often go downstairs to look at all the rancher and cowboy types in their cowboy hats, boots and western outfits.

Because of our curiosity about anything to do with cowboys, my brothers and I enjoyed watching cowboy western shows. One of our favorites was *Bonanza*, which we watched every Sunday with our grandfather. The show was about three brothers named Adam, Hoss and Little Joe Cartwright, who lived with their widowed father, Ben, on a ranch called the Ponderosa.

"It is important you respect each other, just like these brothers respect each other," my grandfather would say while we were watching *Bonanza*.

At first, I didn't understand what he was talking about. Every week the three brothers were fighting, and here was my grandfather, saying we should be like them!

After watching many shows, I began to understand my grandfather's lesson. Although the brothers would fight with each other at home, whenever a brother was in trouble outside the home, the other brothers and their dad would soon come to his rescue.

I remember the first time I took my grandfather's advice. I was eight years old in Mrs. Way's third grade class. One day, a student knocked on the classroom door. Mrs. Way asked me to come to the front of the class.

"Miss Dinkel wants to see you," she said. Miss Dinkel was the principal of our elementary school. I thought I was in trouble for something I did.

I was afraid of Miss Dinkel, ever since Mrs. Way brought her in because our class was misbehaving. When she entered the room, she was carrying a big strap—it was brown and had a thick black stripe running down the middle. Mrs. Way warned us that Miss Dinkel slept with her arm propped on a pillow, so it would be well rested to use the strap on our hands if we misbehaved again.

I followed the student who came to my class, but he did not lead me to Miss Dinkel's office. Instead, I was led to my brother Lewis's first grade classroom.

Miss Dinkel was there. So was Lewis. And there was Leung, who was also in the first grade and the son of one of the waiters at my grandfather's restaurant. My brother and Leung were the only two Chinese students in the class.

Immediately, I knew what was going on. My brother and Leung were always fighting each other, so they must have been at it again. It got to a point where our mom and Leung's mother were yelling and screaming at each other to defend their sons.

Up until then I never thought about defending my brother, like the way the Cartwright brothers defended each other on *Bonanza*. I wanted to help my brother by telling Miss Dinkel that maybe Leung had started the fight, but I said nothing.

There were two small chairs at the back of the classroom. I began to sit down on one of them.

"No, you stand over here," said Miss Dinkel, pointing to the floor. Then she sat my brother and Leung down on each of the chairs.

Miss Dinkel towered over both of them. The other students

turned around from their desks to see what was going on.

"I want you to translate for me," said Miss Dinkel as she nodded at me. "If you two ever fight again, I will punish both of you," she said to the two boys.

As I did the translation, I did not look at my brother. I spoke directly to Leung.

"If you ever fight again, this lady will kill you," I said in a calm voice, as I spoke to him in Chinese.

Miss Dinkel was pleased because her message instilled a look of fear in Leung's face. The two boys never fought again.

○   ○   ○

In Grade 3, Mrs. Way asked me to show-and-tell about the twelve animals of the Chinese zodiac. At first, I didn't even know what that was. I asked my mom and my grandfather. They didn't know either. Eventually, Mom asked one of the cooks in my grandfather's restaurant. He listed the twelve animals of the Chinese horoscope, which I read for show and tell to my class. It was then that I realized that people were interested in my Chinese background because I was the only Chinese kid in the class.

One day when I was nine years old, my grandfather said he was going to make some Chinese medicine. He had a large, ten-gallon ceramic vat, which was located in a narrow room where he kept his valuable papers, including his immigration and head tax records. He also stored his suits and other clothing there. This room smelled of mothballs, and it was lit by one dim bulb. Nevertheless, this room was sacred, because it was considered Grandfather's Room.

My brothers and I watched as my grandfather began making his medicine. He put bags of Chinese herbs into the vat. Some of them looked like bark and were of different sizes and shapes and had pungent, funny smells. Then he put in what looked like slabs of meat, a chicken and a whole dried snake. I didn't know it at the time, but he also stuck in a beaver.

There were two cases of gin near the vat. He opened each bottle and started pouring in the gin. Then he got me and my brothers to help him fill the vat with gin. Once the vat was full, my grandfather picked up the lid, put it on the vat, and sealed it with tape.

At some point after the vat was sealed, my grandfather communicated to us that he had put a small beaver in the vat. I can't exactly remember how he told us this—maybe he pointed to the beaver on the Canadian nickel—but I wanted to see the beaver for myself. As an adult, I've often wondered how he got someone to bring him a beaver for the medicine vat. Most likely the beaver was found on the banks of the Highwood River, just outside our hometown. But as a child, my only curiosity was to see what the beaver looked like.

.Periodically, I would ask my grandfather when the medicine would be ready. But in time, I forgot about the beaver in the medicine vat.

Three or four years later, my grandfather unsealed the vat. He refilled the empty gin bottles individually with a funnel by scooping the liquid with a pan. The liquid was now a dark colour and had a strong medicinal smell. This tonic was going to keep my grandfather strong and healthy.

After filling all the bottles, my grandfather gave me a large jar filled with clear liquid and a dark object in it. It was the beaver. It had all its fur and appeared to be almost black from soaking in the Chinese herbs.

My grandfather told me to take the beaver to school and give it to Mr. Ray, who was the junior high school principal and eighth grade science teacher. The students, who were two years older than I, gathered around to look at the object in the jar. It probably would have qualified as the most unusual thing anyone brought to school for show and tell—except that I didn't tell anyone what was in the jar.

○　○　○

Sometimes when looking at family albums, it's not pictures that are in the album that tell a family's history, but rather the missing pictures that tell the real story.

I started putting together my album when I was six years old. It contained the usual assortment of pictures found in albums— pictures taken at Christmas, pictures of family, pictures of students in my classes in elementary school from grades one through six.

When one of my brothers brought a girlfriend to our house in

Vancouver about fifteen years ago, she wanted to look at our family pictures. Even though I had moved out of my parents' house by then, I still kept my album in the bedroom I grew up in. I brought out the album for everyone to see.

As my brother's girlfriend went through the album, she saw a picture of me and my brothers with a man in a group photo.

"Is this your dad?" she asked, pointing at the picture. No, it was Uncle Dick in the picture with us.

She looked at another picture of us with someone else.

"This must be your dad," she said. No, it was a picture of us with Uncle Mak.

As she went through the album, I realized I had no pictures of my dad in the album. I felt rather embarrassed about this and could not look at my dad. My mom looked on but said nothing.

Later, Mom brought over some pictures, which she told me to put in the album. One was a picture of their wedding in Hong Kong in 1954, and the other pictures were ones with my dad in it. I had seen the wedding picture before — it was a copy of the one on the table in my parents' bedroom. Although my dad looked like a Chinese movie star, his face was expressionless. He was wearing a custom-made suit from the Hudson Bay store in Calgary. My mother had a smile and a look of optimism, wearing an American-style outfit made in a Hong Kong tailor shop just before their wedding. The people at the tailor shop were not treating her well because she had just come from rural China. So my dad said a few words of English to impress the staff and make them believe that he was wealthy from living overseas, even though he had earned just enough money to get married.

The year before, my dad had worked as the head cook in a busy restaurant called the Grill Café in Kimberley, B.C. Kimberley was a mining town, and the workers came from the mine to eat at the restaurant. My dad earned $85 per month, which was three times what he got at his previous job as a cook in Calgary. When I was growing up, he would always talk about Kimberley nostalgically because there he was able to earn enough money to go to Hong Kong to marry my mom.

One image I had never seen while growing up, either in pictures or in real life, was my father crying. He said he had shed enough tears for a lifetime, after the mother who had adopted him died when he was twelve years old. He had been kidnapped from northern China and adopted by his mother in southern China when he was three years old. When my grandmother adopted my dad, she did so without consulting my grandfather. Before my grandmother died from cancer, she might have written to my grandfather to ask him to sponsor my dad to come to Canada. After she died, my dad lived on the streets and with different relatives in China.

My grandfather sponsored my dad to come to Canada in 1949, perhaps more out of obligation than love. My dad arrived in Canada just before Christmas that year. He recently recalled that he was washing dishes on Christmas Eve. He remembers being in tears because he couldn't understand why he was working when everyone else was celebrating Christmas in my grandfather's restaurant.

When I was growing up, my dad always stopped me from crying. I often thought he felt my tears were not worth crying compared to what he went through. I also wondered if he did not celebrate my achievements because it made him feel inferior. He did not go to my high school and university graduations. For many years I had felt anger. But we never released our emotions in front of each other.

I had heard from my mother and brothers over the years that my dad had cried in front of them. One time was when he thought he was about to lose the restaurant he operated in Vancouver. Another time, after he sold the restaurant, one of my brothers saw him shed tears because he thought he would never get hired again as a cook.

In June 2004, I organized a trip to Kimberley for my mom, dad and two of my brothers. My dad wanted to visit Kimberley for their 50th wedding anniversary.

When we arrived in Kimberley, my dad didn't recognize any of the streets or where the Grill Café restaurant was located. At first we were told the restaurant had burned down. Then we were told by someone else that the sporting goods store was now located where the restaurant used to be. Finally, we found the restaurant. It had been partially burned down, then rebuilt and is now a German restaurant called the Gasthaus Restaurant.

I took pictures of my parents in front of the restaurant and also in front of the Kimberley sign with the giant cuckoo clock. After hearing my dad talk about Kimberley for so many years, I had finally felt that it was a part of my history.

I had the pictures developed a week after we got back from our trip to Kimberley. I had one of the pictures enlarged and bought a frame for it.

I remember the moment I gave the pictures to my dad. It was at the front foyer inside his house on Father's Day. He always had a hard time thanking me for anything. This time was no different.

As he turned around and proceeded up the stairs, I followed. All of a sudden, his knees grew weak, and I thought he was going to fall down. Then he started to cry.

"I am very happy. First, when your brother took me to China, and now you taking me to Kimberley," said my dad in Toisan.

I patted my dad on his shoulder. I wanted to cry, but I could not.

Christmas with my grandfather, Gan Seto. Beside my grandfather, from the left, are my brothers Lewis, Hopman, Hopland, and myself. This picture was taken in the residence upstairs from Grandfather's restaurant, the New Look Café.

My brother Wayne in the 1970s. Because Wayne is my youngest brother, he can only recall meeting our grandfather once, after we moved to Vancouver.

My parents in Kimberley in 2004.

My parents' wedding picture in Hong Kong in 1954.

AUTHOR'S NOTE

My Grade 7 English teacher, Mrs. Maureen Kinzell, encouraged me to write short stories, even entering me in one writing competition. Since the competition was about farm equipment safety, I failed miserably because I grew up working in my grandfather's restaurant and knew absolutely nothing about farm equipment. At the time, I didn't feel like I had anything of importance to write about.

I signed on for the workshop so I could write down some of the stories that had shaped my life. During the workshop, our facilitator, Brandy Liên Worrall, made the observation that what I am offering is a unique perspective of growing up Asian Canadian in a small prairie town.

My family history begins with my grandfather coming to Canada from Canton, China as a head tax immigrant in 1910. He sponsored my dad to come to Canada in 1949. Later, my dad saved enough money to go to Hong Kong to marry my mom.

I hope to write more stories, beyond those of immediate family members. These include stories about uncles, aunts and other people I have encountered in Alberta and British Columbia.

By looking back, I can move forward. The structure of the workshop has helped establish a framework for my storytelling. The workshop is great for anyone wanting to write their family histories and stories, even those who don't think of themselves as writers.

I consider myself very fortunate to be part of the first-ever CCHS Family History Writing Workshop. I really appreciate the input and support of everyone in my class. We shared many moments of inspiration, camaraderie and insight.

My background: I graduated from SFU majoring in business adminstration. My work life has mainly been in sales and marketing, as well as stock market trading. Hobbies and interests include ice hockey, dragon boat competition and maybe now, short story writing.

~Dan Seto

Three Voices

A Wong Family Album

Hayne Wai

My kindergarten graduation, 1953.

HAYNE, DECEMBER 1952

When he left the couch, my brothers and I would wait until he left the room, and then scurry over to where he had been seated to see if any coins had dropped out from his pockets. We made sure we looked under the cushions for our potential bounty.

This is my earliest recollection of my maternal grandfather. Gong-Gong was in his eighties, and I was only five years old when we arrived in Vancouver from Hong Kong to stay with him and Pau-Pau, my grandmother. He seemed tall, but then to a five-year-old, every adult was. His hair was thin and white and swept back, and he walked slowly. Gong-Gong smoked a pipe, which he would light with a crack of a match from the box at the side of his couch. I had my first whiffs of aromatic pipe tobacco. It smelled good then, and it still does now.

Gong-Gong had this round watch on a chain in his pocket, unlike all the other watches I knew, which were worn on one's wrist. When he spoke, I never knew what he was saying in his *Sayyup* dialect because I only knew Cantonese. But that was oblivious to him. He talked at me and my brothers as if we did know what he was saying, expecting us to be obedient. Gong-Gong was a retired merchant who was living out his senior years at the house he and Pau-Pau and their family had lived in since the late 1930s, at 713 East Georgia. And now my four brothers and I had come from Hong Kong to join them.

The house was dark and cold. It was December, and for us boys, it was our first chilly winter in Canada. The stairs going up to our bedroom were creaky, windy and steep. In the kitchen, the stove fascinated me because it had to be lit by newspapers and sticks of wood, and more matchsticks. I watched curiously as Pau-Pau lit the fire, and then lit her cigarette with the same match.

Rice and Chinese sausage were regular fare at 713 Georgia, along with salted fish, and Pau-Pau's specialty, steamed ground pork with salted duck egg. She was able to pass on this village recipe and others to my mother. For breakfast, they gave me something I had never tried before. It tasted different but okay. It was corn flakes with milk. But I let it be known that I preferred rice with raw egg to begin the day.

Downstairs in the basement was even darker and colder, and that's where the furnace was. There was a large heap of black hard stuff I had never seen before. I was told not to play with it because it was dirty. Uncle Bill would shovel that stuff into the furnace and get the fire going—and again there were those matchsticks.

One day, Pau-Pau asked me to go to the corner store to get some cigarettes for her. It was only half a block away, a safe distance then, even for a little boy like me. She taught me to say "Export," and showed me the brand of cigarettes she smoked, a green box with a woman on it. "Export," "Export," "Export," she repeated, and I can't remember what I said but it came close, I think, to "egg-sput." I had arrived in Canada with just three words of English—"yes," "no" and "ten." The final word I had just learned from my oldest brother Joe before we left Hong Kong.

Off to the corner store I went with the coinage she placed in my hand. I crossed my first street all on my own, opened the store door, entered, and there was this older woman behind the counter. "What would you like?" she asked in Cantonese. "Cigarettes for my Pau-Pau," I replied. "What kind?" she asked. I froze for what seemed like minutes but were probably only seconds. I did not have the courage to try to pronounce "Export." I did the next best thing—I pointed. "That one, the green package," I said, my finger aimed at the package with the woman on it.

I went back home, mission accomplished, but never told Pau-Pau that her first English instruction for me had failed. Not because of her, but because, as I suspected, I would be a slow learner with this new language. But that was about to be addressed as I was to be enrolled in kindergarten, the Good Shepherd Anglican church over on Keefer Street a couple of blocks away. There, my first teacher, Miss Sawbridge, would help me learn the alphabet.

My recollections of kindergarten are scarce, but I remember it as quite different from the few weeks of kindergarten I had at St. Stephen's School in Hong Kong. There, I was driven to the school, and I remember lots of playmates and games. The major difference was language; many of the other kids spoke English, although I found some Chinese-speaking classmates. I spent most of the time trying to figure out what Miss Sawbridge was saying. When I didn't understand, which was often, I just gave her a quiet smile and pretended that I did know.

The alphabet was a major educational goal for me. I came home one day having learned A to E and excitingly telling Aunt Rose. Unlike my mother who grew up in Hong Kong, Aunt Rose grew up in Vancouver, spoke English well, and would help me with my alphabet, as well as reading, 'riting and 'rithmetic during my first years of school.

On graduation day, we got to wear a cap and gown, and walk nervously to the podium to receive our certificates while flashbulbs captured every step. This was followed afterwards with group photos in the church courtyard. There I was, at age five, cap and gown, proudly holding my certificate of accomplishment, as I had learned the entire alphabet. Everything was picture-perfect, except for my shoelace, undone, loose, waiting a mishap, and captured by the camera. It seems that while I had accomplished mastering the alphabet, my skills at shoelace tying were lacking. Thank goodness that was not a criterion for graduation.

PAU-PAU, AUGUST 1939

They would have set sail for Hong Kong from San Francisco today, after having taken the train from Vancouver. I was quite sad to see them go last week, but I've got their wedding photo here in my hands. It was taken at our home. I've never seen her so happy before — she is just elated! And why not, it was her wedding day. Every girl should be happy on her wedding day, not anxious like me when I got "married."

My eldest daughter, Fok-lan, married that young man from Hong Kong that she's talked about ever since she came back from there four years ago. I had to leave her there when she was nine years old for several years. It was not an easy decision, but it was the best for her given our family situation. She grew up separated from the rest of us. I don't think it has impacted too much on our relationship. I hope not anyways.

She met this young lad there when she was a teenager. He drove a fancy car, lived in a huge house, and his father had a large business. Since she came back, they have corresponded regularly while he went to university in London. She told me a few months ago that he would be coming to Vancouver. Then he asked her to marry him, and afterwards, they would return to Hong Kong. She's had a big smile on her face ever since.

I am so glad that she is marrying by choice. I never had that option. At sixteen, I was matched to this forty-two-year-old merchant from Gold Mountain. I wasn't so sure I wanted to marry him, but there was little choice. He was successful and looking for a wife to bear him children. I had heard of Gold Mountain. It was a very far distance away, traveling weeks by sea, but many others from the villages had gone there already.

It would be good to have a family, I said to myself then, as I never knew mine. How much longer could I continue to play the harp, sing, and perform with my "aunt" and "uncle"? We have moved around constantly, to Malaysia and Singapore, but I was tiring of that. They would arrange for me to be in a good place, I was sure. But what if I didn't want to marry him, could I really say no? I met my husband-to-be for the first time on our wedding day. It was all arranged through a broker in Hong Kong.

But fortunately, everything has worked out. Twenty-five years later, we have five children, my husband lives with me, and he is proud of our family. We have gone through much turmoil, and we lost our eldest a few years back. But things are stable now. And now my eldest daughter has married. She is the happiest I have ever seen her. This makes up for all the years I had to leave her overseas.

For her wedding, the Chinese minister from the local United Church performed the ceremony in our home. It was a small gathering, only a few friends and family, but lots of laughter and excitement. My sons, James, Gilbert and Bill, were all dressed up in their very best, as was my husband. Rose, my youngest daughter, looked so pretty in her dress. This is the way weddings should be—fun, with family and festive—very different from my own, which felt more like a business transaction.

This young man from Hong Kong she married—he's a bit slim but polite, good-looking and extremely charming. He will provide well for her, so I will not have to worry. I am told he speaks with an English accent because he's been in London for the last few years. My husband thinks he's a bit formal, but that's how these Hong Kong people are. My sons, they grew up here so they don't really know this Hong Kong style, but they've taken a liking to him. He sticks out a bit here in Saltwater City with his mannerisms and such.

They should be in Hong Kong in a couple of weeks after stopovers in Hawaii and Shanghai. They hope to send for me soon to visit. I look forward to that because I haven't been back for many years. In fact, the last time I was there, I left Fok-lan behind with relatives. I sense that she looks forward to returning to Hong Kong with him, that lifestyle is still a part of her.

I hope things will be safe there for them, as there is much talk of Japan invading more of China.

Photograph courtesy of author.

My parents' wedding picture. Front row, from left: my mother, Pau-Pau, Gong-Gong, my father. Back row, from left: Aunt Rose, Uncle James, Uncle Gilbert, and Uncle Bill.

UNCLE JAMES, SUMMER 1943

Well, at least she didn't cry, that would have been terrible to take. I don't think I could have faced her crying again. Dad, well, I was quite surprised to see him at the station. He just aloofly shook my hand, but I could sense a touch of anxiety in him. He never shows emotions, Chinese dads just don't. He quietly slipped me a few dollars and calmly said, "Keep well."

I'm on the train now, off to Edmonton for basic training, along with my best buddy George. There are others from Chinatown on board who also enlisted—Roy, Doug, Harry and Dan. We're all excited about this new adventure for us. It's kind of scary, but it's also going to be fun.

When I told Mom a couple of months ago, she took it pretty hard, but Dad, he was kind of okay with it. But like I said, he never shows emotions. Mom, she just shook her head and said, "Don't go. They don't treat us well, and we don't owe them anything. I can't afford to lose you too. Your first commitment is to family, and you're the eldest." Then she burst into tears, and I had to leave the room.

It wasn't an easy decision to enlist. God, I might get killed or something! But we've been talking a lot about it in the community. There are those who say that since the government won't allow us to vote, get decent jobs, become citizens, or allow family members in, what do we owe them? They treat us like second-class citizens here! While some of the white people are our friends, most don't like us, no matter how well we speak English. There are so many restrictions on us—on where we can sit in theatres, when we can go bowling or swim at the Crystal pool, the only indoor pool in town. It's just not all that safe to walk around many parts of town for a Chinese. At election times, those white politicians use us as their targets to get elected.

But it's still our country, even if we're not treated well. We want to have a future, good jobs, and families. We want equal rights and recognition as Canadians. If going to war for a country that denies us these basic rights is the way to achieve them, then me and my buddies, we'll do just that. Because when we get back, they're out of excuses, and then they'll have to get us the vote and treat us better. Also, China is really hurting—those Japanese have killed millions, and our homeland is being destroyed. They took Hong Kong almost two years ago—that's where my sister and her husband are, and we haven't heard from them for months.

There have been a lot of meetings in the community. We've

each made up our own minds. Some won't go—but me, I'm going. I'm twenty-four, and I'm at a crossroads. This is my ticket for the future. I want to be trained as an airplane mechanic. I hear they want gunners, but I'm not that crazy, they get killed awfully fast. That's why they're looking to recruit more gunners. Yep, a mechanic, with skills I can use when I get back, to get a good job, help the family, settle down, maybe have a family of my own.

I need the veteran's benefits to get an education. When my older brother died a few years back, I had to quit school to support the family. I missed out on my education. I need training, and the benefits will help. Otherwise, I'm stuck with these low-paying jobs that the whites give to us Chinese.

You know, I think I'd look great in a uniform! Girls like guys in uniforms, I know that. It'll be a great way to catch their attention, but then I've never had trouble catching their attention. My sisters tell me I look like Robert Taylor, the actor, but I think I'm more like Errol Flynn!

The way I figure this, maybe by the time I get through basic training, this war will be over. Hey, I'll get to walk down Pender Street in my uniform! And then we'll walk down Hastings Street to Granville. It'll be interesting to see how the whites react to a group of Chinese guys in Canadian uniforms downtown. Maybe then we can sit in movie houses wherever we want.

My mom, she took time off from her sewing job to see me at the station. As I said, thank God she didn't cry again. I think that would have done me in. My younger brothers Gilbert and Bill and my sister Rose were there too. I asked them to take good care of Mom for me. I know they will.

My buddies and I, we've grown up together, enlisted together, and we're going to all come back together. And now, George has just begun the poker game. "Hey guys, I'm in!"

"The most difficult sentence to write about your family history is the first sentence. But once you've written it, you'll ask yourself why you waited so long to begin! Why didn't you start earlier?" That was a key message I picked up from a speaker sharing his family history Power Point presentation at the Japanese National Nikkei Museum in June 2005. That did it — I had procrastinated too long. I went home and wrote my first sentence that evening, and then began tracing my maternal grandparents' family history in Canada.

My grandfather Wong Wah arrived in Victoria at age sixteen in 1884, and my grandmother joined him in 1914. They had six children, including my mother who was born in 1917. My brothers, sister and I were all born in Hong Kong and came to Vancouver in the early 1950s. I knew I could eventually track down many of the key dates and facts, but something was missing — that was how to bring family history alive, with personal stories and human emotions beyond the standard family tree chart.

When the Chinese Canadian Historical Society offered a family history writing program, I knew it would be a great opportunity to develop the skills to make my family history come alive. I had little experience writing narratives but rather my background was in turning out streams of reports and briefing memos. Years of poor English grades in school and university had convinced me that I could not write creatively. It was time, I decided, to get over these barriers and participate in the workshop.

My thanks to Brandy Liên Worrall, our instructor, who was very helpful in articulating ways to make our writing fresh with the sounds, flavours, sights and emotions experienced by family members. Our workshop group supported each other not only on the written technical feedback on drafts, but also with empathy, understanding and suggestions in our search of our family history.

There remain many challenges in tracing family histories, but that should not hinder the confirmation and validation of our family and community experiences. I hope that my stories will encourage others to write that first sentence of their own family history. Once you begin, please don't stop! Our family histories are too important for us to leave untouched, unwritten, and unshared.

~Hayne Wai

The Legend of Lore Neen

THE LIFE OF MY GRANDFATHER

Candace Yip

He probably didn't look like an educated man to the people who got on and off the elevator at the Paramount Building in downtown Victoria. If they had bothered to look closely, they may have noticed that his black jacket was rumpled and shiny from wear, that the collar and cuffs of his white shirt were frayed and yellowed, and that his fingernails were dirty. He barely nodded as each passenger entered through the accordion-pleated steel doors of the elevator and called out his or her floor. If they had tried to engage him in conversation, they would have come up short. He was lucky to have the job, even though he spoke little English. He probably rode up and down, from floor to floor, without uttering a word. Talk about a dead-end job. He was going nowhere, opening and closing the elevator doors at each floor without getting off.

How, then, did he pass the interminable hours? Did he daydream of being back in China where his education in a Taoist temple or Buddhist monastery prepared him for the life of a scholar? The skills that he brought with him—calligraphy, brush painting, poetry, "kung fu"—were of little use to him in Gold Mountain. "For Hire—Classical Scholar with experience operating elevators," his calling card might have read. He lived long enough to see both professions become obsolete. Sadly, he did not live long enough for me to know him, except through his calligraphy and painting and through the family stories that have been, dare I say, "elevated" to myth.

In 1994 I traveled to Hong Kong for the first time and visited my uncle, William K. Lore, a solicitor and retired naval officer, who had lived with my grandfather in Victoria in the 1920s. I was astonished to learn from Uncle Bill about my grandfather's education and the circumstances which led to his family's flight from China to Canada:

Your grandfather's early life from the age of about ten was spent either in a Taoist temple or Buddhist monastery for safety, as my father and his next younger brother had joined the anti-Ching Dynasty rebels after the Tai Ping Rebellion was crushed. They eventually fled China as political as well as economic refugees. Your grandfather learned to read and write in the monastery and became an accomplished scholar and "Kung Fu" expert.

Why was I hearing this for the first time? None of his six children had known anything about his life in China. Strong, silent, taciturn—my uncle's description of him matched the photographs in our family album. My eyes grew wider as Uncle Bill related the following account of grandfather's legendary strength:

There was a meeting attended by my father between the Chee Kung Tong and Kuomintang to resolve their differences with a neutral party present on the top floor of the Chinese Benevolent Association in Victoria. Your grandfather and I were at Lore Yuen Sang together with other family members and friends when suddenly, a friend rushed in to report that the Kuomintang were armed with metal rods and knives and that he feared for my father's safety. Without uttering a word, your grandfather left immediately and later brought my father (grandfather's older brother) back unharmed. Witnesses at the meeting told me that the fighting had already started when your grandfather arrived, and that my father and Lee Mung Kao, the leader of the neutral party, were trapped at the north end of the hall. Without hesitating, your grandfather waded into the crowd, sweeping the combatants aside with his arms, and escorted my father and Lee Mung Kao out of the hall unscathed.

Some years later, while I watched your grandfather smoothing out a table-sized sheet of thin Chinese paper for his calligraphy, I asked him how he had acquired the strength to push armed men aside at that meeting. He replied, "By doing for many years in the monastery what you see me doing here—smoothing out sheets of paper, one at a time with the palm of my hand." When I asked him why he didn't just use an iron to get the wrinkles out, he looked at me sternly. "The iron would change the nature of the paper. It must be smoothed by the controlled warmth of heat from the palm of your hand."

Perhaps my grandfather dreamed of climbing mountains as he rode the elevator to the top floor of the building. Years ago, my mother came across a clipping that she had saved from a Victoria newspaper. There was a photograph of some Chinese characters painted on the face of Mount Douglas. The bemused columnist speculated that the painting may have been the work of Japanese patriots attempting to signal a message to invading ships or airplanes. Myth and mystery aside, my Aunt Victoria remembers trudging up the mountain behind her father, with a heavy pail of whitewash, the climb seeming to be without end.

My mother had taken ballet as a young girl, thanks to my Aunt Victoria, who took a job after school in order to pay for the lessons. The eldest of six children who lost their mother early in life, Victoria took on a nurturing role with her younger siblings and particularly encouraged my mother to develop her talent for dancing and choreography. Victoria, herself, was an accomplished painter, and my Uncle Abraham, the youngest in the family, could play piano beautifully, by ear. They all came by their artistic abilities honestly. Their father—my grandfather—Lore Neen, was a scholar, a poet and an artist, but he was ill equipped to parent and support six motherless children after the death of his wife in 1921 or 1922 (no one I know is certain about when exactly she died). And so he entrusted their upbringing to his older brother and his wife who already had a blended family of ten children. Despite the deprivation that my mother and her siblings endured, they never went hungry and never lacked for exposure to both Chinese and North American culture.

O   O   O

Looking through an old album of my mother's, I came across a treasured photograph of my mother and her three sisters posing with a group of performers in what appear to be Chinese opera costumes. In the very middle of the troupe sits my Aunt Victoria, flanked by my mother, Mary, on her right and by her sister, Louise, on her left. On the far right in the middle row is my mother's baby sister, Helen. My mother had scribbled "1932" at the bottom right-hand corner of the photo frame, which would make her fifteen years old at the time. It is a formal portrait of the theatrical troupe of twenty-one boys and girls, taken by "L.B. Hong" of Victoria. I remember having seen the photo many times before as a child, each time marveling at the fanciful headdresses, especially the one on the boy in the back row that reminded me of Mickey Mouse.

Two of the older boys are wearing fake beards of coarse, white horse hair, suspended between their ears, obscuring their mouths and hanging down to the middle of their chests. Another two boys sport bishop-like crowns, and the boy in the centre of the back row has an ornate, five-pointed crown, similar in shape and size to the one worn by my Aunt Victoria. Looking at the elaborate crowns and the exaggerated, flowing, bell-shaped sleeves of the costumes worn by my mother and her two older sisters, I would guess that they played the roles of queen and princesses (or courtesans) to the majestically clad fellow in the star-shaped headdress in the centre of the back row.

All of the headdresses in the photograph, my mother said, had been made by my grandfather. By her account, there was nothing he could not create—from paintings to poetry, kites and oyster sauce. How wonderful it would have been to have him make me a jewel-encrusted, gold-tasseled crown for my fairy princess costume, instead of the flimsy tinfoil tiara my mother had brought home for me from her New Year's Eve party. He passed away when I, his only granddaughter, was just six months old. He had been living with us when I was born. According to my mother, he would wait patiently for me to wake up. He described my tiny movements in the bassinet as those of a little worm, my head stretching up slowly and receding back into a cocoon-like shape, over and over again. I have always kept that keen observation of his in my memory as an expression of his love for me.

If only he had lived a while longer. Then I could have known, without being told by others, how much he loved children, how he would go to auctions and come back with treasures for the family, everything from pocket watches to sacks of clams for a seafood feast—how he would take the children to English movies and laugh with them in all the right places, even though he spoke no English.

There are so many unanswerable questions. Did he think himself a failure as a father? Did he daydream of going home to a China that existed only in his memory to mitigate the mindlessness of his job as the elevator operator at the Paramount Building on Douglas Street? Apart from hearsay, I know him only through the black and white images of an unsmiling immigrant, the black and white painting of a pine tree that hangs on my living room wall, and the yellowed books of poetry written in the beautiful brush strokes whose meaning I cannot decipher.

On one of my visits to Montreal in the seventies, I casually mentioned to my cousins that I, the only granddaughter of Lore Neen, did not possess a single work of his art. I knew from my mother that grandfather had lived with relatives in Montreal and Toronto and as payment for his keep, had given them paintings. My cousin, Simon, the son of one of the ten cousins my mother grew up with in Victoria, took pity on me and graciously parted with the painting of the pine tree that now sits in my living room. Actually, he gave me two paintings, owing to my grandfather's frugality. There is another painting on the other side of the paper which I cannot see, unless I dismantle the picture from its frame.

I recall being told how he used to write on the bark of trees because paper was so precious in China. The painting itself is a study in economy. A lone pine tree bends gracefully to one side with only three branches bearing needles. Five or six stalks of bamboo spring from the foot of the tree, their shape and direction suggesting a gentle breeze. In the arc of the pine's bent trunk are three rows of calligraphy, the meaning of which escapes my illiterate eyes.

What this spare, black and white painting says to me about my grandfather is that he loved nature and hated waste. He was known for not wasting words, paper, food, time, or his talents as a teacher, scholar, poet, and painter. That he continued to teach, write and paint in his adopted country, despite the lack of appreciation of his work and status as a classical scholar, speaks to me of heroism — not the extraordinary heroics of rescuing his brother from an armed confrontation, but the everyday heroism of working at a menial job to put food on the table while maintaining and instilling in his children a love of nature and the desire to create beauty.

My grandfather, Lore Neen, in Vancouver in the 1940s.

Pine tree with bamboo— the only painting of my grandfather's that I own.

The portrait of the Chinese theatrical troupe, 1932. Second row, third from the left, is my mother, Mary; her sisters Victoria and Louise; and at the end of the second row, on the far right, is her sister Helen.

Just after I signed up to participate in the inaugural CCHS Family History Writing Workshop, my husband and I attended a performance of the play, *No Great Mischief*, at the Vancouver Playhouse. It chronicled the history of a Cape Breton family who traced their beginnings in Canada back to the Battle of the Plains of Abraham. It was the Scottish highlanders who first scrambled up the banks of the river to meet the French in battle under General Wolfe, who remarked that it would be "no great mischief" if they were sacrificed in battle to win the war. The four brothers, descended from these warriors, were heroic in their own sphere when, in the blink of an eye, their history changed course as their parents fell to their deaths through a hole in the ice. What I liked about this family history was its elevation to myth and its connection to the history of the country. It was not unlike my own family's history which, due to revolution and repression in China, was transplanted to and took root in Canada.

My grandfather, Lore Neen, came to Canada as a political and economic refugee. Family members have told me that he was a scholar, poet, and artist, who was schooled in a monastery or temple, and therefore, a "Kung Fu" master. Others have told me that he was a ne'er-do-well with a disheveled appearance. My goal in taking this workshop was to learn how to reconcile these disparate visions of my grandfather and to connect him to both the larger historical events and the smaller personal gains and losses in China and Canada that shaped his life and artistic expression.

Of his six children — Victoria, Martyn, Louise, my mother Mary, Helen and Abraham — only Victoria and Louise are still with us. At my Aunt Helen's funeral on April 29, 2006, six of my cousins urged me to put pen to paper and record our family's history for our generation and the next. My first university degree was in Honours English, and I am a lawyer by profession, while all of my cousins have science or business degrees. To them, I was the logical choice for family historian. In any event, the timing was perfect. I was about to begin the workshop, which has given me the tools, techniques and tenacity to keep researching, writing and revising. With Brandy's guiding hand and the support of my fellow family historians, I am ready to flesh out the Lore family history.

~Candace Yip

Luc Gai

FAMILY DINNER AT SIXTH AVE

Gail Yip

My grandparents' house on Sixth Ave.

Mommy says that we are going to leave earlier today to go to Ma Ma and Ye Ye's because Uncle Fong has come out from Spirit River for Christmas. I don't know where Spirit River is, but I know that it is far away and that he is a doctor there. He always gives us nice Christmas presents. I wonder what I'm going to get this year.

If Uncle Fong is there, then Uncle Bill and Auntie Winnie and the kids will be coming from Victoria. It is going to be a big party! I wonder if we are going to have to kowtow to Ma Ma and Ye Ye. I always feel silly when I do that, but then we always get money in little red envelopes from them. I'll hold Wendy's hand since she's little. Will Mommy be wearing that pretty shiny jacket?

Why do I always have to sit in the middle between Wendy and Carol in the back seat? I never get to sit by the window, so I can never see anything. All I can see is my shiny black shoes and the blue fuzzy dots on my new party dress. I wonder if I can touch the ceiling. Daddy says not to touch the ceiling, or we'll get in trouble. Can he see my hand trying to reach up? He says he has eyes in the back of back of his head, but I think he's lying. Are we there yet? Finally!

Ma Ma is looking out her bedroom window. I can see the attic above her bedroom. We aren't allowed in the attic—it is haunted up there.

Ma Ma is so little. I wonder if I am bigger than her now. She can still sit in the baby high chair. I can't, my bum is too big. I hope she lets me sit in her rocking chair today.

The gate is always so hard to open! I want to ring the bell on the front door, but I think it is broken. Even Daddy can't get it to turn so it must be broken.

Ma Ma is opening the door, and she is giving us all big hugs. Wait! There it is on the windowsill—the blue can with the cheese cookies! I wonder if Ma Ma is going to give us any this week. They are my favourite! Will I get in trouble if I stand on her sewing machine and try and reach the can?

Ye Ye is probably sitting in his chair in the living room smoking a cigarette. I wonder why his fingers are always yellow. Why is he always dressed up in a suit? Does he ever wear blue jeans like Daddy?

I want to slide down the railing like Ricky, Dennis and Martin, but

Mommy says it's not ladylike because everyone will be able to see my panties. Then Carol will sing, "I see London, I see France, I see Gail's underpants!" Should I slide down the railing? Maybe not—I might rip my new dress. I know what—I'll pretend I'm the bride coming down the stairs!

I wonder why there are those wires along the ceiling. I can pull them and pretend I want to get off the bus.

Maybe I'll go upstairs to see if I can find where the ghosts are. Maybe I can find the door to the attic today.

Oh, there's Ye Ye smoking his cigarettes. His ashtray is full of cigarette butts. I would sure like to stick my fingers in the sand and pick out the cigarette butts.

Oh, look at all the presents under the Christmas tree! I wonder who that big one is for? I wonder how many are for me. Who decorated the tree? Ma Ma has lights just like ours.

I'm going to see if my red egg is still there. Ma Ma's buffet is just like Mommy's, but ours is whiter. There's my egg! I'd sure like to open the door and touch it. It's got my name on it, so it must be mine. So if it has my name on it, why can't I take it home?

I hope we get to play elevator today. It's fun to open and close the door and pretend we're going up and down just like in the stores. I hope we don't get yelled at today for being too loud.

Are we going to eat soon? I am so hungry! Did Ma Ma make bread stuffing? I don't like it—it tastes funny. I hope the gravy doesn't get on the corn, then it tastes yucky. Are we having Jell-O for dessert? Cherry, I hope. Where's everyone going to sit? Everyone is talking all at once. It's too noisy in here!

O   O   O

There were twenty-nine members of the Law Clan if we were all able to get together for Christmas dinner in the years before Ma Ma died. Ma Ma and Ye Ye had six sons, four daughters-in-law, one daughter and one son-in-law. There were nineteen Law grandchildren, but three were born after Ma Ma died of lung cancer, possibly from secondhand smoke, in 1961. With so many people present, there were always a lot of clamor and lively conversation. Having no brothers, I found my younger male cousins rather boisterous. I remember how I hated going to visit Ma Ma and Ye

Ye's on Christmas Day because we had to leave our new toys that we just got from Santa.

Approaching Ma Ma's house, I could see the gate, which was the metal type typical of the era and now in vogue once again. It had an unusual latching device, which I always had trouble opening—probably a good thing as it kept us grandchildren from escaping. Though the front yard was not very big, it was always well manicured and lush. Ma Ma grew snapdragons and marigolds in a small narrow flowerbed in front of the fence that defined the property line. I especially remember the strong fragrance of the yellow roses. We would pick the thorns off the bushes and stick the flat side to our foreheads.

There was always a mass of colour during the hot days of summer, and the perfume lingered in the air. Ma Ma had a large Chinese vegetable garden on the side and back yard. One vegetable that especially sticks in my mind is "gow choy." I used to wonder, How can a dog be a vegetable? Or is it a number nine vegetable?

Ma Ma was a slight person. Her feet were bound when she was young, so they were very tiny. She wore fur-lined handmade moccasins which had an Indian motif embroidered on the top. They were only a child's size thirteen. What amazed me most was her ability to sit in the high chair that was there for her visiting grandchildren.

I cannot ever remember speaking to my Ma Ma or her talking to me. I did understand Chinese when I was a kid, but having a conversation with her completely eludes me! Even though there was a language barrier, Ma Ma enjoyed watching bowling, *The Honeymooners* and *The Bob Cummings Show*.

Ma Ma's rocking chair was in the kitchen beside the stove. Ma Ma would sit there knitting for hours. Whenever she dropped a stitch, she would place a safety pin on the stitch and wait for Mom to do the repairs during our weekly Sunday visits. We were always warned not to stand too close, or we would get our feet caught under the chair while someone was rocking. My sister Wendy and I used to rock together until the other cousins wanted their turn.

Today, whenever I eat Hawkins Cheezies, it conjures up memories of the eight-inch baby blue cardboard can on Ma Ma's windowsill. This cylindrical container held cheese-flavoured sandwich crackers that had a creamy cheddar cheese filling and a waffle-like surface much like the cones found at ice cream stands today. Ma Ma probably bought this type of cracker thinking that there would be enough to go around amongst her grandchildren. Once emptied, the can became a storage container for her sewing supplies.

We received many wonderful Christmas gifts from Uncle Fong, who owned the drugstore in Spirit River. For many years Uncle Fong was the only doctor there. My cousin Eldonna remembers, "There was no x-ray or other equipment. He operated with a gifted pair of hands and lots of guts." During his thirty years of practice, Uncle Fong delivered upwards of 2,000 babies.

Mom once told me that his nurse Alice, who later became my Auntie Alice, would choose the gifts for all my cousins. I had visions of Alice going to the shelves in the drugstore and picking something special for each of Uncle Fong's nieces and nephews. Those of us who were close in age would receive the same gift but usually in a different size and colour.

I can recall the "Baby Ben" alarm clock he sent me when I was about seven. I felt very grown up at bedtime when I pulled the stem out to set the alarm. This was a nightly occurrence until Christmas 1962, when I received a clock radio from my parents. I now had to remember to switch the dial to "auto" for the radio to awake me at seven o'clock each school morning. It was much more soothing to start my day with the voice of a radio announcer than to be awakened with a shrill jangle that started my heart pounding.

When meal time arrived, we were all able to sit in the kitchen. My aunts and uncles sat around the kitchen table, while the grandchildren were relegated to the "kids table." Christmas dinner was traditional Western style with all the trimmings. Mom cooked the turkey at our home and then transported it to Ma Ma's. Ma Ma made sausage and bread stuffing, which was not to my liking at the time. Now, I can't get enough of it. We also had cranberry sauce, mashed potatoes and gravy, and corn. For dessert we would usually have Jell-O, Christmas cake, and shortbread.

When dinner was over, my cousin Christina washed the dishes, while Carol and I did the drying. I was always too short to put the dishes away, so I would stack the newly dried dishes on the counter.

Darlena, Christina's younger sister, had the job of sweeping the floor. I don't remember my cousins Roberta and Linda or my sister Wendy helping with any of the chores. The male cousins definitely never lent a hand.

After dinner, the kids watched *National Velvet*, which was on at 7:30, but the big event of the evening was *The Ed Sullivan Show* at 8 P.M. Since the antenna reception was very poor, Ed Sullivan monopolized the only three channels we could receive. I came to hate that show with a passion.

Around 8:30 P.M., we would start getting ready to leave for home. Uncle Lum and Auntie Lucy were usually the first to leave because they lived in Cloverdale. The kids were dressed in their pyjamas because of the distance they had to travel to get home. I knew it was time to go home when I heard Uncle Lum say in Chinese, "Get your shoes on!"

Ye Ye and Ma Ma.

Author's Note

I started "digging" for my "family roots" about this time six years ago. After twenty-two years as a volunteer coordinator for a child safety programme, I decided to hang up my hat and devote more time to family history. The bulk of my writing had been formal correspondence to school principals, coordinators and volunteers throughout Burnaby. The extent of my non-business letter writing was my annual Christmas letter and emails.

"What will my family do with all this material after I'm gone?" This is the question I asked myself as I sorted through all the photocopied documents of ship's lists, Chinese immigration registers, census records, city directory pages and other bits of information I thought was relevant to my research. The question now was how to put it all together without sounding like a report with only names and dates, which would put the reader to sleep.

When the Chinese Canadian Historical Society offered this writing program, I hesitated. I looked at the course content and found it rather daunting. But then I overcame my inhibitions and have never looked back.

With Brandy's and all my classmates' encouragement and advice, I have been able to make my memories come alive. Once I got started, I couldn't stop. My classmates even offered to sell me some of their "blank pages" in this publication! I hope to continue writing.

The narrative I have written is about my childhood memories of Sunday dinners and family gatherings at my grandparents' home in Vancouver in the late 1950s. My grandfather was eight years old when he and his parents, who owned a mercantile and labour contractor business, had settled in New Westminster Chinatown in the late 1890s. Ye Ye made at least three more trips across the Pacific and in 1913 returned to New Westminster on his final trip with my grandmother and two toddler sons. Between December 1916 and June 1928, five more children were born. Sometime in the late 1940s, they moved to 25 East Sixth Avenue in Vancouver.

I would like to say, "Write and keep writing even if it is only for yourself." One day in the distant future, your descendants will thank you as you have made their family history come alive.

~Gail Yip

Collecting Cranbrook

MINING GRANDFATHER'S PAST

Ken Yip

My only connection to my paternal grandfather was a huge, old portrait that hung above the fireplace in the living room of our farmhouse from when he was probably in his fifties. He was quite handsome, dressed in a three-piece western suit with a striped white shirt and Windsor knotted striped tie. Other than having a strong resemblance to my father, he was a mystery to me. However, the portrait didn't always hang there. I remember when my younger brother and I used to play at the far end of the living room, riding our tricycles. One day, my father began constructing a small bedroom where our play area was, and shortly after, my grandmother came to live with us along with the large portrait.

All the time I was growing up, I never thought to ask my grandmother about him. My father never spoke of him, as he was only three or four years old when my grandfather passed away. As I began researching and gathering information, I started to assemble a sense of connection with the man in the portrait. I discovered that he must have been someone who was hardworking and driven to better himself. He was able to build a business and become a respected merchant in the small town of Cranbrook, which enabled him to start a family.

○   ○   ○

My wife and I decide to go on a road trip to the east Kootenays where my grandfather settled and where my father was born. Extrapolating from census records, I discover that my grandfather was probably only sixteen when he decided to leave home and make the journey to Gold Mountain — *Gum Shan* — in search of his fortune. Armed with the research I had done, I retrace the area around Wild Horse Creek, near Fort Steele, where my grandfather prospected and mined for gold and eventually settled. With only hand-drawn maps from an 1890s issue of *BC Prospector* and archival maps of Wild Horse Creek and Fisherville, we leave the main highway and start down a dusty gravel logging road that is barely wide enough for a logging truck.

Sections of the road have washboard ruts, so travel is slow. Several sections are cut through rock outcroppings with a sheer drop-off and no shoulder. Even with checking the maps several times, we manage to miss the turn-off to Wild Horse Creek. I turn the vehicle around at the next widening of the road, executing a precarious three-point turn.

Locating the turn-off, we venture down what must have been an old wagon road that is overgrown with tall grass and brush. Only two wheel ruts are visible like two ribbons cutting through the tall grass as they disappear into the brush that is nearly ten feet tall. With the grass scraping the undercarriage of the SUV as well as the encroaching brush on the sides of the vehicle, we manage only a slow crawl. There are sections of the wagon road where the ruts are filled with water or mud.

As we begin to climb, the vegetation becomes sparser and travel now proceeds a little more quickly. We finally come upon the Wild Horse Creek Cemetary. We pull over to have a stretch break and stroll through the grave markers whose names have long since disappeared. Very few markers remain, as most were made of wood. The whole cemetery is shaded by a tall canopy of trees and is badly overgrown. A few plots have wrought iron fences that poke up through the tall grass. With the filtered sunlight and the odd shaft of bright sun, the feeling is surreal yet peaceful.

We continue on past the remnants of Fisherville, a boomtown that sprung up overnight and disappeared just as quickly when the gold strike petered out and the townsfolk began ripping up the floorboards and boardwalks for gold dust that had fallen through the cracks. Finally, we arrive at the area marked on the maps as "Chinese Sites." The claim sites are packed very close together, no more that twenty-five feet wide, along what was the riverbed. I stop the vehicle and get out. Part of my search is complete.

I stop and take in the moment, trying to imagine that I am standing in front of my grandfather's actual claim. I can hear the sound of the pick axes hitting hard rock. I see two Chinese men working as a team. One is sorting and sifting out the large boulders and rocks and piling them in neat rows forming a rock wall. The other is shoveling the loose gravel into the sluice box and pulling the lever to let water into the box to wash away the sediment, leaving the few miniscule grains of fine gold dust glinting in the sun. Although the yield is meager, there is a look of satisfaction in the faces of the two men. The work is slow and painstaking but enough to give hope.

Looking at the meticulous rows of tailings left at the abandoned claim sites gives me a sense of the perseverance required to eke out a living in my grandfather's times. To walk in the very footsteps of my forefather is an incredibly moving feeling. My next phase of research at the Fort Steele archives may allow me to determine the actual location of the claim sites where he worked.

Next, we go to downtown Cranbrook, along the street where my grandfather and father both walked. Although the street name has changed and the original buildings of Chinatown are long gone, I feel my third-generation connection. Durick Avenue, now Sixth Street, is where my grandfather had a general store. I stand on the sidewalk and look down the street to the train yard, where my grandfather received his sale merchandise. I stop at the office of the Cranbrook Historical Society and speak with several local historians who provide me with a few grains of information and records of where my grandfather had been buried in the Cranbrook City Cemetary.

○ ○ ○

Cranbrook became a major hub city for the east Kootenays due to the railroad. In its prime Cranbrook had two opera houses that brought in major North American musical theatre productions and current headline vaudeville stars of the day. Cranbrook even had two newspapers that were printed twice a week, the *Cranbrook Herald* and the *Cranbrook Courier*.

We pay a visit to the Cranbrook city archives, hoping to find an obituary for my grandfather in one of these newspapers. The archivist helps me locate the issues of the newspapers for the time period I am searching. Each issue is anywhere from twenty to twenty-five pages long. I move down through the chronologically arranged stacks until I find the two issues for the week preceding my grandfather's date of death, March 23, 1925.

I feel like I'm about to begin an archeological dig. I scan each page slowly, column by column, looking for obituary notices that are scattered, without rhyme or reason, as fillers for the main stories or articles. The newspapers are densely packed with news from around the world to just around the corner, informational articles, almanac predictions, fictional serials and ads of local merchants. The main section for obituary notices is "Local News" for Cranbrook and surrounding communities, near the back of the paper. The "Local News" section not only records births, accidents, illnesses and deaths of people and livestock, but the comings and goings of the prominent members of the community. Obituaries are typically only a few lines, with only the briefest of details. The more prominent the individual, the longer the notice. I find several Chinese listings along with native Indian ones.

As I'm scanning, I keep getting distracted by the some of the stories. I am reading about the rounding up of an African elephant, the last of the wild animals that escaped from the circus that came to town two weeks ago. Another recounts the wonderful evening of song and dance from the Belle Starr musical revue. These little vignettes help break up the monotony. They give an interesting glimpse into life in my grandfather's time.

I scan past my grandfather's date of death by two weeks, and I'm really disappointed that I haven't been able to find any mention of him. I cannot believe that his passing was not recorded in some way.

Undaunted, I make a second pass. I am not leaving until I exhaust every effort. To my great surprise, I come upon an article on the front page of the Thursday, March 26th, 1925 *Cranbrook Courier*, titled "Chinese Merchant Buried Monday" that contains his name: Yip Chung Ben. The article is nearly an entire column in length! I had been looking for only a small two- or three-line entry. I cannot believe my great fortune! I sit back to read the story, savoring every word.

The article begins with his arrival at Galbraith's Ferry in 1882, as Fort Steele was known then. It chronicles his exploits as one of Wild Horse Gulch's first known Chinese placer miners, to market gardener, to successful general merchant. The article talks about his business partner, Dennis Quong, who was as devoted as a brother. He is associated with my grandfather for nearly forty years, beginning with when they worked mining claims together.

I read the article again and let the words transport me to the day of my grandfather's funeral. On that Monday afternoon, the sky is overcast, and the air is crisp and cold. A long procession of thirty cars, bearing mourners, "Chinese and whites alike," slowly winds its way along a gravel road to the Cranbrook cemetery. The somber procession is accompanied by the discordant sound of native Chinese musical instruments played by Chinese musicians dressed in long white robes and headdresses. At the rear of the procession is Cranbrook City's Home Town Band. The clash of the two musical cultures gives the procession a festival-like atmosphere, leaving onlookers curious. The lead car, ahead of the hearse, bears an enlarged portrait of my grandfather that is mounded by floral Masonic and societal emblems and huge wreaths of cut flowers, along with bowls of oranges, preserved fruits, mushrooms and other traditional Chinese foodstuffs, as offerings to deities and ancestors.

As the mourners assemble at the graveside, the casket, barely visible, is draped with floral arrangements, and the large portrait is placed on a stand near the altar. A silence settles in as the mourners wait for the service to begin, only broken by the occasional sniffle and stifled cough. The principal mourners standing nearest the casket are my grandfather's wife and young son — my grandmother and father — and his business partner. My grandmother, holding her son's hand, is visibly feeling the loss, as is the business partner. A riveting eulogy is given by an elder of the Chinese Freemasons, recounting my grandfather's accomplishments and his legacy. As a sign of respect for the white mourners, the minister of the Methodist church delivers a powerful and moving sermon, which is interpreted by a Chinese elder of the church. A long procession forms as the mourners file past to pay their last respects.

I reread the article several times as I picture myself there at the ceremony, sharing not only in the grief, but also in the great respect and support being paid by the whole community to the memory of my grandfather. The feeling of extreme pride knowing that my grandfather was a well respected and an important member of the community continues to fuel my quest to find out more about him. The article gives me a sense of connection for the man depicted in the portrait, who has been a mystery to me all these years.

The portrait of my grandfather.

Chinese Merchant Buried Monday

Deceased Was Placer Miner on Wild Horse Creek in 1882—Had Many Friends in District.

A link with the stirring past was severed on Friday of last week when, following an illness of two weeks, Yip Chung Ben, a Chinese merchant of this city and a former placer miner of Wild Horse Gulch, died in his residence on Durick avenue.

Yip Chung Ben was, with the probable exception of Lee Jack, a countryman of the deceased who still clings to his old home in the once rich gulch, the oldest of the Chinese miners of the past century. He came to Galbraith's Ferry in 1882 and had closely identified himself with the life of the district up to the present day as placer miner, market gardener and general merchant. Associated with Yip Chung Ben for the past 38 years, first as a partner in his mining claims ,and also in his business ventures, was Dennis Quong, another Chinese as well known in the district as was the deceased himself. Nowhere in British Columbia could be found two more devoted partners than were Yip Chung Ben and Dennis Quong, nor two who trusted each other more implicitly. Dennis is feeling the loss of his old partner keenly, as is to be expected after a close association of nearly forty years. The surviving

I am a third-generation Chinese Canadian. I've spent the last thirty-five years writing technical reports and analyses as a clinical engineer working in healthcare. I remember receiving a provisional pass from my UBC English 120 professor, if I swore never to take another English course ever again. He was taking pity on the engineering students in his class. I have stayed true to my oath until the CCHS Family History Writing Workshop.

My family history focuses on my father's side, which has only two main characters: my grandfather and my father, both of whom had no other siblings. At first glance, it seems the task would be simple, but I have found it to be very challenging, both in gathering what scarce information there is and then deciding what to do with it. My research has given me pride for my grandfather, who was an early pioneer in the East Kootenays, and for my father, who had a part in a pivotal event in Chinese Canadian history. In order to honour their memory, I must pass this history on to my sons.

This workshop has enabled me to take an extraneous collection of information, both historical data and social histories, and allowed me to craft a narrative about my grandfather that is both informative and interesting! I intend to continue writing about my father's efforts during the Second World War as part of a Special Forces unit in Burma.

The workshop format is invaluable through feedback from both the instructor and fellow participants. The techniques have allowed me to break down what appeared to be a daunting task into small bite-sized pieces that I can continue to build on. The exercises have given me a way to focus and tease out even more memories and information, and to make connections that I had not appreciated or thought of before. The workshop has intensified my sense of pride for my ancestors.

~Ken Yip

AFTERWORD
Finding Ourselves in History

As I read these poignant and evocative stories that have come out of the Chinese Canadian Historical Society's Family History Writing Workshop, I am reminded of the importance and power of family history in understanding our collective past. Long before the history of nations such as Canada and the United States, history as a way of understanding our links to the past was primarily "family history," in the sense of imagining ourselves tied in unbroken chains to the ancestors who preceded us. Our understandings of ourselves are so powerfully shaped, for good or ill, by our relations to family and to others who have raised us. For those of us fortunate enough to hear stories passed down as family lore, whether we treasure them or not, we should recognize that they form an incomparable inheritance, different and unique to each of us. I am deeply impressed by this inaugural volume that has come out of the first workshop—I am reminded that it was out of a desire to understand my own family history that sparked my interest in becoming a historian, and that the long journey through graduate school and my apprenticeship as a professional scholar has brought me back again to that very beginning.

I was born and raised in Canada, and was fortunate to know as a child my Goong-Goong, my grandfather Yeung Sing Yew, who paid $500 (over a year's salary at the time) in Head Tax as a thirteen-year-old migrant in 1923, months before Canada passed the Chinese Exclusion Act which forbade any further Chinese immigration. His father before him had come to Canada to help build the railroads, and his older brothers were pioneers in B.C. who worked in mines, grew produce, owned grocery stores, and built lumber mills. He followed them in their pioneering activities, and then for over thirty years, my grandfather worked as a butcher on CPR ships that cruised between Vancouver and Alaska. My grandfather lived almost his entire life in Canada, only returning to China to marry, and was forced to leave his pregnant wife behind in China because of Canadian Exclusion laws. These generations of split families were the direct legacy of Canadian legal racism. His own father had left him and his brothers in China as children because he could not afford to bring them over until they were old enough to work and help pay off their own Head Tax payments.

When my grandmother and mother were finally able to join my grandfather in Canada, just before I was born, it was an emotional reunion. She had never known a father growing up, and he had been deprived of knowing his own child—my mother was twenty-seven years old the first time she met her father in 1965.

Perhaps he took a special interest in his grandchildren because of what he had missed: I remember walking as a four-year-old with him to Chinatown and his pride in showing off a grandchild to his friends. Most of them had lived a similar life, and the look of joy in their faces as they gathered in the café to play with me spoke volumes about their own missing children and grandchildren. Some of them were able to bring their wives and children to Canada after the Immigration Act of 1967 made it easier to reunite families (the large wave of Chinese who came to Canada in the 1970s contained significant numbers of these family unifications), but many of them lived out their days in Chinatown flophouses as lonely old men, bereft of wives because immigration policy had kept Chinese women out, and blocked by racism from having relationships with white women.

Just before the publication of this volume, the Prime Minister and Parliament of Canada officially apologized for imposing the Chinese Head Tax. I think it is entirely right that Canada as a nation formally apologizes for its treatment of men like my grandfather and his friends. It is long overdue, since the movement for such an apology is almost half a century old, and if it had been made in a timely fashion, many more of those who paid would be alive to hear it. I wish my grandfather had lived to hear Canada say, "We are sorry." As a child, I remember him showing my mother his Head Tax certificate and explaining the years of hard work it took him to pay it off. He knew it had been unjust, recognizing that nobody except the Chinese had been required to pay, and an apology while he was alive would have had immeasurable meaning. He knew the racism that had singled out the Chinese—he lived it every day of his life as a second-class citizen in Canada—but materially he knew it as he struggled to repay his debt.

But the apology is only a symbolic step, and this volume of family stories is a much more important, concrete example of what we still need to do in order to right our nation's wrongs. Our national history still excludes the Chinese, just as our national policies did, recognizing them only for being here during the Gold Rush and helping build the trans-Canada railroad. What were they doing the rest of the time? My grandfather, like his father and brothers, lived and worked in Canada during the rest of that time, helping build it under incredible duress. Most European settlers came to the West coast of North America to find the Chinese already there. Before the railroad, it was easier for the Chinese to cross the Pacific in a ship than for Europeans to cross North America. The irony of the Chinese helping build the transcontinental railroad is that it made it easier for trans-Atlantic migrants to come to the Pacific coast. Our standard Canadian history is still wrong. The story we usually hear is that anti-Chinese agitation centered around the claim that the Chinese came late and "took" the jobs of whites. In fact, the complete opposite was true. Anti-Chinese movements began as European settlers arrived to find Chinese, First Nations and others (such as Japanese and South Asians) well settled in a Pacific British Columbia. The rhetoric was that the Chinese "took" jobs away from "whites"; the reality was that "whites" wanted to take jobs away from the Chinese who were already there, just as they wanted to take the land from the First Nations people who were already there. For four decades on CPR cruise ships such as the *Princess Patricia*, my grandfather served those who recently arrived from Britain and Europe. They had the privilege to instantly call themselves Canadian and to imply that he and not they had just arrived. But he knew, and we must now remember, that the life he made here, as hard as it was, was a life made in Canada.

The rise of the anti-Chinese movement in Canada created a lingering history of government-sanctioned exclusion and racism. Unlike the difficulties faced by other migrant groups to Canada, including many European settlers who faced prejudice and discrimination, the Chinese and other Asian migrant groups faced legalized racism enforced by the full extent of Canadian law and state power. This is a crucial difference that many Canadians still do not understand when they dismiss the "complaints" of Chinese Canadians asking for a recognition of past wrongs. "My grandparents faced racism too" or "Nobody forced them to come to Canada" become ways to dismiss the call to recognize what was done to the Chinese. But there is a great difference between the vast array of exclusions and disenfranchisement of anti-Chinese laws and the all-too-common forms of discrimination that many other migrants to Canada sadly had to face. One illustration of this difference is to remember that the $23 million collected with the Head Tax would be worth well over one billion dollars in today's currency, and that during the almost four decades when the Head Tax monies were split between the Canadian and British Columbia governments, it provided B.C. with a significant portion of its early public revenue (remember that income tax did not exist until the end of World War I). The proceeds from the Head Tax paid for roads and funded schools and hospitals. We all live with the historical legacies of white supremacy in the form of legal policies such as job discrimination, immigration exclusion, and the revenue generated from the Head Tax. We have all either benefitted or suffered from this history in the forms of privilege that it granted or denied our ancestors, and the legacies of the inequity did not go away with the death of my grandfather, his brothers, nor his friends. Even newcomers to Canada cannot protest that they were not around when these inequities occurred. We are surrounded by the material legacies of injustice, in the form of buildings and roads and everything purchased with those millions of dollars of tainted money. Our collective responsibility cannot be assuaged by an individual's recent entry. A good analogy would be to think of the financial responsibility of a collective entity such as a corporation. If you buy shares in a company and it turns out that the company was being sued for a toxic leak that poisoned a large number of people, it does not matter that the leak occurred before you bought your shares. When you bought ownership in that company, it meant that your share price would reflect the financial damages that the company now owed. You cannot argue that your shares should be exempt because somehow the company that existed before you bought the shares was a different company than the one you now owned. Canada's history, good and bad, is all of our collective history.

Ironically, the surveillance and discrimination that the Canadian government enforced has unintentionally created some unexpected benefits in the very detail of the records it collected on the Chinese. The fact is, the Head Tax collectors kept meticulous records of those who had paid. Recently, I was at the Vancouver Public Library showing a CBC camera crew how to use the microfilm records there to look up relatives who had paid the Chinese Head Tax. They were filming a story on how the Head

Tax Redress movement had spurred a rush of people to the library to look up ancestors, sparking a renewed interest in the lives of Chinese Canadian pioneers. For those descendents who had been handed down the original Head Tax Certificate that served as the official receipt that their ancestors had paid, there was no need to consult the microfilm records. But for the vast numbers of those who did not have the original certificates, the records at Vancouver Public Library were the only way to find official proof that their relatives had indeed paid. Needing someone to demonstrate the challenges of using the microfilm, the CBC crew asked me to look up my grandfather while they filmed. When the story aired on CBC news that night, I saw myself pretending to scroll through the records of those who paid the Head Tax, searching patiently amidst the cursive longhand of the government clerks for my grandfather's name. On TV, finding his records took less than five seconds; in real life, it isn't that easy. The General Register of the Chinese Head Tax contains almost 100,000 Chinese names; however, they are not listed in name order but chronologically according to when each person entered Canada and paid the Head Tax. In other words, even if you know the exact year when your grandfather or father entered Canada, you will still be scrolling day by day through the thousands of Chinese who entered Canada each year between 1885 and 1923. The comprehensive nature of this vast list of names, oddly enough, is of great benefit to those who are interested in tracing their family history. Here is the perversity of legislated racism — the government's desire to charge only the Chinese the onerous Head Tax meant that they kept track of every Chinese migrant to Canada between 1885 and 1923, giving us an unparalleled set of records. For those who were welcomed into Canada, no such historical documentation exists. If your ancestor stepped off a boat in Halifax from Scotland during that same period, he or she walked off the docks with nary a trace left in government records.

Fortunately for the CBC camera crew, I already knew the exact page of my grandfather's registration entry. But for those who are searching line by line through the register, it is an arduous task precisely because there are so many names. It was partly because of the extreme difficulty of using the microfilm that I became involved in a project with my colleague Peter Ward at UBC to create a digital index of the Head Tax Register that would be searchable not only by name, but by any of the categories of information that the

Canadian government collected—village and county origin, port of entry, name of the ship, even height. The creation of this digital index is an arduous task in itself: it will take almost three years for our researchers to enter line by line each of those tens of thousands of entries, but at the end we will have an unprecedented database that can serve as the spine for the history of Chinese Canada, a comprehensive list to which other records can intersect.

There are numerous difficulties with such a list, of course. The first, and revealing, problem is that many of the people named in that list are not who they say they are. My grandfather Yeung Sing Yew, for instance, appears in the records as Low Jang Yit. The Chinese Head Tax legislation not only charged a year's salary for entering Canada, it restricted entry to those who were direct relatives of those already in Canada. My grandfather and his brothers could not prove legally that they were the sons of my great-grandfather despite the fact that they really were, and so they each had to buy legal papers that showed they were the sons of someone else already in Canada, in my grandfather's case switching his family name from Yeung to Low. Despite being brothers in life, on paper they were not legally related. My grandfather acquired this "paper" identity from a family friend, a fictive existence which he carried for the rest of his life in Canada—it eventually appeared on his seaman's certificate, on his passport, on his retirement cheques, on every piece of English language mail that appeared at his door. The first time I ever saw my grandfather's real name in English, I glimpsed the strange shape of its letters on his headstone through tears of mourning.

The difference between Yeung Sing Yew and Low Jang Yit signals more than just the distinction between real name and paper identity. The difference is also between two ways of knowing history, of understanding our connection to the past. Yeung Sing Yew indicates a family history, a way of knowing my Goong-Goong through relations of intimacy and family memory, conveyed and spoken through a shared language of duty and love. Low Jang Yit, in contrast, is written in the cold and bureaucratic language of surveillance and hate, the spiteful words of a border guard mentality. Historians for so long have treasured the wrong side in this war of words. As scholars we covet government records, holding them up as the gold standard of historical truth and dismissing family history as the faulty memories of the elderly and befuddled. Archives are filled with the scribblings of government clerks, eschewing oral history for so long as a flawed document of the past, full of mistaken memories and biased recollections. But which is the more dangerous bias and the more egregious mistake? Is not Low Jang Yit the name written for all that was cruel and unjust about our nation's racist policies toward the Chinese? Should we not instead speak of Yeung Sing Yew — brother, father, and grandfather? Which life is worthy of being remembered and incorporated into a shared past of which we can all be proud?

The two names need to co-exist, of course, both historically and in our present memory, because to remember one at the expense of the other is to forget a truth that should not be forgotten — either a truth about the inequities of the past visited upon the present, or an equally true but oft-neglected story about ancestors who toiled in silence, telling their lives if they speak to us at all in the whispered voices passed down orally around kitchen tables and in family gossip. What a tragedy that both professional historians and so many of us in our daily lives neglect to listen to such haunting voices, forgetting the truths they utter until they are quieted forever, lost to the lies that are written to bolster the celebrations and triumphs of national histories.

I have my Goong-Goong's death certificate, issued by the British Columbia provincial government after he died in August of 1978 when I was 11 years old. Several months ago, my mother gave it to me so that I could trace his name more easily in the records of the Chinese Head Tax Register. It sits, folded in an envelope on my shelf, near the photo I have of him when he was young, the same age that I was when I graduated with my PhD in history. The photo was taken in 1937, when a fundraising drive collected money in Vancouver Chinatown for the relief of a China just invaded by Japan. In the photo he is tall and thin — the Head Tax Register listed his height when he entered Canada as a remarkable 5' 9$\frac{1}{2}$", tall not only for a thirteen-year-old but even in comparison to the adult men who stepped off the Empress of Canada with him on February 26, 1923. This photo was taken not long after he returned from China, a newly married man leaving behind a pregnant wife. He could not have known that he would not see his family again for twenty-seven years. Why else would he be smiling, the same smile as the photo taken in 1965 when he was finally reunited in Canada with his wife? The two photos sit beside each other on the shelf that my wife built as an ancestral altar. It's not like the altars you see in most Chinese houses, with incense sticks and framed portraits of unsmiling elders. Our altar has a lot of smiling faces, capturing the moments of happiness that I prefer to remember.

Photographs courtesy of author.

My grandfather, Yeung Sing Yew,
Vancouver Chinatown, 1937.

My grandmother and grandfather,
reunited in Canada, 1965.

Between the smiling photos of him in 1937 and with my grandmother in 1965, I have precious few images of my grandfather during those years. There is a gap, lost to photographic recall just as those years were lost to the possibility of creating memories of a family life unlived. I remember as a child how he would watch me as I bounced up and down on his knee, as if he were trying to capture in his mind's eye decades of memories, catching up for years forever gone. When the Canadian government and Canadian society began to correct the injustices they had served upon its Chinese Canadian citizens, one of the wrongs they righted was to allow those like my grandfather who were forced to buy false papers in order to enter Canada the opportunity to rectify their names. This "confession" programme was not without its problems, because even if there was no retribution or punishment for someone admitting that they had an illegal identity, each confession could implicate others in the tangled web of truth and lies that anti-Chinese legislation had created. But in his death certificate, at least, both of his names sit side by side. "Yeung Sing Yew," his death certificate reads, "a.k.a. Low Jang Yit." I look at his death certificate, and I see not just his two names, his two histories, but all of our rich shared history, documented and undocumented, written by government clerks or spoken by family members. And so in the lives and deaths of those who came before us, we must find our common history, lest we forget some essential truth of our past and lose the ability to share a collective history that we have made together.

As a scholar, I believe we need a redefinition of Canadian history to finally address the central role played by those who were heretofore erased or written in the margins of our official history. One of the reasons I became a scholar was because the history I learned in school was so at odds with the reality I knew from family stories passed down from my grandfather and great-grandfather. Their Canada was not just a story about railroad workers and victims of racism. They told stories of Chinese men who had children with First Nations women, who lived and traded among aboriginal and European migrant communities in rural areas throughout B.C., who operated cafés and grocery stores in small towns throughout the Prairies, who lived and worked together with their neighbours to create Canada. I also knew the stories of my grandmother, mother, and father, who came later to a changed and different Canada. Like those who came before them, these later waves of Chinese migrants do not fit into easy generalizations. Some, like my parents, were university-educated and professionals, the products of modernization in China, Hong Kong, and Taiwan. Others fled nascent nationalist movements in Southeast Asia and Latin America, or simply chose to continue journeys begun by their forebears, tracing complicated paths not from China but through generations of other overseas Chinese who had gone to Australia, New Zealand, Peru, Trinidad, South Africa, Mexico, the United States, Vietnam, Cambodia, the Philippines, Indonesia, Malaysia, Thailand, India—every part of the world.

What is inspiring about this collection of family stories is how they illustrate the rich diversity of our collective past. Judging from these eight wonderful pieces, the CCHS Family History Workshop was more than a success—it serves as a model for how we should write and study history. Our shared past needs to be in the hands of more than just professional historians, it needs to be shaped by all of us together. The Authors' Notes at the end of each story should be treasured, for they reveal the courage it takes to first put pen to paper, to begin the process of making history. They offer the hope that all of us—even engineers like Ken Yip told by professors never to write again—can create poignant stories that ring with human truth. For so long, Chinese Canadians were made to feel less than Canadian, their history ignored. This collection shows the lie in that exclusion. What a powerful model they present for reimagining Canada—that we are all more than Canadian, connected to an extraordinarily rich history that spans the globe. These stories remind us that the strength of Canada as a nation is that its peoples bring together a diversity that overflows its borders, are shaped by the wider world and, at our best, are capable in turn of shaping for the better that wider world.

~HENRY YU

Professor of History
University of British Columbia

Founding Board Member
Chinese Canadian Historical
Society of British Columbia

About the Editor

BRANDY LIÊN WORRALL is a writer, editor, book designer, and community arts events organizer. She is currently in the MFA in Creative Writing program at the University of British Columbia and was the associate editor of *Amerasia Journal*, the premier journal for Asian American Studies, published by UCLA. She is working on a series of memoirs about her Vietnamese and Pennsylvania Dutch families. She lives with her two children, Chloe and Mylo, and her husband Henry in Vancouver, British Columbia. Visit her press at **http://www.lulu.com/rabbitfool**.

About the Chinese Canadian Historical Society of British Columbia

Registered under the Society Act of B.C. on May 18, 2004, the Chinese Canadian Historical Society of British Columbia (CCHSBC) is a broadly based membership society with educational goals. Our main objective is to bring out the untold history of ethnic Chinese within the history of British Columbia. We achieve this through sustained efforts at document preservation, research, family and oral history promotion, public education programmes, an active website, and many other initiatives.

One such initiative is the establishment of the Edgar Wickberg Scholarship for Chinese Canadian History. In honour of Edgar Wickberg's vision in creating the CCHSBC, his continued commitment and dedication to its goals, and his many years of teaching students at the University of British Columbia, proceeds of this book will help grow a scholarship fund for encouraging education and research on Chinese Canadian history.

For inquiries about supporting this scholarship fund and the overall goals of the CCHSBC, or to become a member, please email **info@cchsbc.ca** or visit **http://www.cchsbc.ca**.